L D

From the Hands of His Enemies
To Serve God Without Fear

EBED PUBLICATIONS
In love, serve one another

By
Johnny Moffitt
with Jimi Miller

Delivered From the Hands of His Enemies, To Serve God Without Fear

Copyright © 1996 by Johnny Moffitt

All rights reserved

All Scripture references are from the King James Version of the Bible.

Published by:

Ebed Publications
P.O. Box 3595
Hagerstown, MD 21742-3595

ISBN 1-884369-33-2

Printed in the United States of America
For Worldwide Distribution

CONTENTS

Chapter　　　　　　　　　　　　　　　　　　　　　　*Page*

1. "I'm here, and I ain't leaving!" 1
2. "My life ain't worth nothing!" 11
3. "Monkey-rum can make ya blind." 21
4. "Yeah, I wanta do that!" 33
5. "This is getting out of hand!" 43
6. "I don't want to go out there." 49
7. "This ain't the place for you." 57
8. "Church? What's her name?" 65
9. "Man, I was wrong about you." 77
10. "What do you mean, accident?" 87
11. "I think we'll just break the date." 93
12. "I like having you home." 99
13. "God, You don't understand!" 105
14. "Go see Alvin Shambeck." 109
15. "How would you like to move?" 117
16. "You sure ain't allowed to cuss!" 121
17. "It says what you said it says." 129
18. "It's from God." 131
19. "She wanted to tell me about a dream." 137
20. "I think God wants us to be involved." 143
21. "Did you call me for money?" 155
22. "Estonia is where I want to be involved." 161
23. "We had to have government contacts." 167
24. "What was your name in the club?" 173
25. "What's the bottom line?" 179

I have known Johnny Moffitt since the night he accepted Jesus Christ. He has changed thousands because he has been changed. His true story will change you.

Morris Sheats, D. Min.
Senior Pastor, Hillcrest Church,
Dallas, Texas

In 1965, for the first time in his 24 years, Johnny Moffitt found something he really wanted to do while watching the same movie four times. The movie was *"Easy Rider."* The thing to do was ride a motorcycle — a "chopper," like Peter Fonda's Harley-74 in the film. That led Johnny to join an outlaw gang of bikers until a freak accident that should have killed him got his attention.
This book relates the chain of humiliating and exhilarating acts of God upon his life that brought him to launch the Worldwide Voice in the Wilderness prison ministry. When God moves in a life, anything can happen.

Chaplain "Ray" Hoekstra
International Prison Ministry

Delivered! That's Johnny Moffitt! Delivered from underachieving in every aspect of life except sin. But God doesn't just deliver a man from! He delivers him to! In Johnny's case, delivered to achieve amazing things for God, from praying with an addict in a corn field, to visiting the Queen's prison in England, to aiding convicts in Jamaica construct a chapel in their prison yard. As a cofounder of the Coalition of Prison Evangelists (C.O.P.E.), I'm proud to be an international joint-venturer with God, with Johnny.

Frank Constantino
Coalition of Prison Evangelists
Christian Prison Ministry
Bridges of America

AUTHOR'S PREFACE

In January 1978, I introduced a man to the Lord Jesus Christ. To the best of my knowledge that man was the oldest prisoner in the United States. At 92, he was serving time for killing one of a gang of boys he could not see when he tried to scare them off his property with a shotgun blast.

The prisoner was locked up in the Colony Farm Prison in Milledgeville, Georgia, and I was there to preach. But before I started, I sat down next to the old man and said, "Tell me about yourself."

For fifteen minutes he poured out his heart to me. When I got up and preached the Word of God and gave the invitation to trust Christ for salvation, he was the first one down to the altar. I glanced over at the chaplain who was bawling like a baby. It was the first time in over two years the old man had responded to anyone.

The inmate got parole and went home a new man, a new creature, a new creation in Christ. He had found the Lord of his life, and I, Johnny Moffitt, an underachiever from the word Go, had fulfilled the ultimate charge entrusted to me. By boldly speaking the eternal truth of the Gospel of Jesus Christ to a small congregation of underachievers, I had rerouted a soul headed for hell.

This is my message to underachievers.

I passed the first twenty-seven years of my life accomplishing nothing, just going through the motions and not really caring. I was unmotivated. I had to go an extra summer to high school before I could graduate with my class. I flunked out of Texas Tech University because I played pool when I should have been in classes. After four years in the Air Force I was discharged and sent home with one stripe, the one I got for Basic Training. I accomplished nothing. I never even received an Article 15 for misconduct. I've lost count of the number of jobs I quit during the years I rode with outlaw gangs in Texas. I never finished anything I started. The only thing I did well was make excuses. I was a good talker.

My father used to say, "Johnny, make something out of your life."

How do you make something out of your life? I wanted to, but I didn't know how. So, just to please him, I enrolled in business college where most of the students didn't like me and I didn't like them. But one of the women students had heard from God. She took her seat at the perpetual-poker table next to my filthy britches and finally got up enough nerve to invite me to church. That's where this Mr. Nobody-Nowhere met Jesus.

During the past twenty-two years since I have been a Christian, for no reason that I know of, God used me to build a multimillion-dollar boys' ranch in Texas to help pre-delinquent and abused youngsters; to found "A Voice in the Wilderness," a prison ministry that is now actively involved internationally; to serve as a member of the International Board of the Full Gospel Fellowship of Churches and Ministers; and to cofound COPE, the Coalition of Prison Evangelists, International, and serve as its vice-president.

I was invited to Dallas to meet with ministers from around the world at the Charismatic Leaders' Convocation, then invited to the Presidential Inauguration for Ronald Reagan. Why should I receive invitations to such meetings? I don't know. It's just God. He opens phenomenal doors.

I have preached in 5-member churches and I have preached in 5,000-member churches. For a guy who had nothing, who did nothing, and for most of his life could not have cared less, the difference is Jesus Christ and the power of God.

Johnny Moffitt
Dallas, Texas
June 1996

CHAPTER ONE

"I'm here, and I ain't leaving!"

Terrors shall make him afraid on every side, and shall drive him to his feet. Job 18:11

1969: Richardson, Dallas, Garland

On a Friday afternoon in September 1969, in the parking lot behind my apartment in Richardson, Texas, twenty-three Harley-mounted Bandidos gunned their motors, waiting for me to make up my mind. Finally, I said, "You guys go on, split. I ain't going."

"Whale, you ain't going?"

"Man, you don't know what you're saying! Labor Day weekend in Austin, man! Homegrown grass! Wine! Women!"

"But Whale, your scooter's already loaded. Whaddaya mean, you ain't going?"

"I ain't going!"

"Okay, okay. Be cool, man. So you ain't going. We'll see ya later. Come on, brothers. Let's git 'n the wind."

It was a rush, hollering loud enough to be heard over the Harley motors revving up, but it was nothing compared to being in my place in the gang, rolling down the road. I really wanted so badly to go, I was screaming inside.

The guys were gunning for the last run of the season—a big run, not just a party. The brothers in Austin had discovered a run-down, deserted farmhouse with

Delivered

five rooms, maybe six, and the guys and their women would be riding in from all directions, in groups or straggling, for a three-day blast. They'd be bringing in the booze—good stuff, good dope, good loud rock and good girls. By Monday the food might be tainted some, but who would care? We cured everything with whiskey.

We would talk about the guys who didn't show up, the ones who got busted on the way, and we'd curse the pigs who confiscated their stuff, then took it home and drank it. More than likely, smoked it. It was always a good feeling, being with the guys, talking about what's going on. They'd be talking about me this time until they started getting it on. All those guys and women, my friends—five hundred, probably—sleeping inside the house, outside on the ground, off in the woods—stepping over people having sex outside in the middle of the day, drizzling beer on them. That's the way we were—it was our culture, our society.

I never could make it in straight society, but I was an officer in this one. I was one with them—acted like them, dressed like them, smelled like them. They were where the action was. We were always either fighting for each other or fighting among ourselves: brothers, but closer than kin.

So, what was I doing staying home? It was because of the accident that happened on a run three months earlier that shook me and brought me down, way down. It happened on a Friday. At midnight about twenty of us, the entire Dallas chapter, had headed south down Texas Highway 75 to meet and party with some of the other clubs at Galveston Beach. There's hypnotic joy, riding with the pack, hearing nothing but the roar of forty big wheels pounding the highway, seeing nothing through the thick darkness except what gets picked up by our headlights—beer cans, cat eyes and an occasional bat

I'm here and I ain't leaving!

darting in and out through the light beams. Bats didn't like the light, and neither did we.

By two in the morning we were ready for a beer break. Our president Chuck, first in line, led us off the road and over the shoulder into the shallow bar-ditch. Tiger and Cowboy, riding double, were second in line and I was third. I should have been second since I was the president's number two man, and they were in front of me only because Tiger was road-master on the runs.

We were breaking out the Coors when two headlights, coming fast over the hill, searched the sky, then zeroed in on Tiger and Cowboy. Without slowing and without swerving, the car crossed the road, jumped the shoulder into the ditch, then slammed dead-on into the half ton of metal and rubber and flesh that was not a hand's breadth away in front of me. I felt the impact and smelled the car as it rumbled over the rocks. I heard Tiger screaming as he hurtled through the air, and my own voice yelling, "Oh, my God! No! No! No!"

As Cowboy flipped wide into the field, Tiger and the 800-pound Triumph slammed into a heap thirty feet away. The rest of us dropped our bikes and crashed through the weeds to the men. Cowboy was rocking and moaning, the bones in his left leg broken in five places. As for Tiger, the car grill had riveted him to the bike peg, then he and the motorcycle twisted and turned through the air as the peg was grinding up through his knee, mangling his entire leg into a bloody mess.

We would counterblast—kill the driver. He turned out to be an unlicensed mental patient who had pressured his mother into letting him drive her car through the country roads at night. Before we could carry out the execution, the paramedics arrived and were inflating plastic buffer bags around the guys' legs. Then the county sheriff intruded himself into our plans by herd-

Delivered

ing us down the road to an all-night grill to cool it over coffee while we waited for the report from the hospital.

The report was that they plastered Cowboy into a hip-high cast and put him into traction, and they cut off Tiger's leg above the knee.

I was no stranger to violence, but that car, missing me by inches, had totalled the bike I could have been riding. That got my attention. I was twenty-six years old, and for the first time in my life that I could remember, I began to ask some serious questions. Why those guys? Why Tiger and Cowboy, and not me?

All summer those questions had stayed with me. Now again they nagged my mind as the diminishing thunder of the Harley motors left me standing alone in the parking lot.

As I turned to go inside, from the corner of my eye I saw the kitchen curtain in the apartment next to mine drop back into place. *Snooping neighbors!* I thought. *My business ain't none of their business!*

I went back into my apartment through the kitchen door and opened a Coors. So, the guys and the mamas were on their way to Austin! So what?

So, it was just my whole life, that's what! I had done nothing apart from them for two years, and I didn't really know why I wasn't with them this time. Spooky! I was muttering curses and kicking trash around on the floor, kicking the garbage can, the chair legs, crying and talking out loud to myself: "What's the matter with you, idiot? What are you doing here by yourself? Why didn't you go? Go on, you can catch them. It's not too late."

I paced the apartment. An infection on my right arm and shoulder was itching, burning, and I twisted my ankle on a beer can on the floor. Furiously, I stomped it flat, then kicked it against the wall where it dribbled beer on the carpet.

I'm here and I ain't leaving!

The shades were down, the drapes drawn against the sun and the neighbors. Who needs them? I locked the door, and reached into the refrigerator, grabbed the bottle of Vin Rose, then circled into the bedroom where I stopped short. What had I gone in there for? Oh yeah, cigarettes.

I couldn't shake the memory of that accident; it had jolted me out of nowhere into a maze of paranoia. I was sweating and itching, and my feet were stinging from the chronic crud I had picked up in Puerto Rico. Puerto Rico! Not even that time the Puerto Rican tried to kill me with a pool cue told me anything like that accident told me.

I smoked a joint, drank some wine, drank a beer, smoked another joint, scratched and paced.

What's the matter with this grass? It's bringing me down!

I sat on the bed, got up, muttered to myself, screamed at myself, called myself names, sat back down. Time flew, then dragged. My mind was in a frenzy, out of control. Something had to give. What do I do now, suicide? Drop out of the gang? That would be suicide, for sure. Nobody drops out.

The telephone rang, and I leaped to my feet. With chest heaving and heart pounding, I let it ring twice. Then, when I reached to lift it off the hook, I saw my hand was trembling. Stupid!

"Yeah?"

"Whale? Is that you?" It was Crazy Willie.

"Yeah, it's me."

"Listen, Whale, I can only make one call, right? Man, we're all in jail, even the girls. They picked us up, and we're only thirty miles out of Dallas. Start 'hangin' paper,' Whale, and get some money down here."

"What did they pull you for?"

"Disturbing the peace, man. Can you believe it? A

handful of 'cowboys' come up, putting the arm on us. We're just defending our rights, and them pigs riding their big fancy full-dressed hogs show up acting tough. Hold it, man. Let me figure something."

Willie stopped talking long enough for my heart to do a hammer roll in my throat. I thought I'd stopped breathing while sweat poured down my back and chest, and soaked my hair.

"Whale?"

"Yeah?"

"You gotta get eleven-hundred bucks. They set bail at forty apiece and there's twenty-seven of us including the women. Oh, and Whale, my bike's at Roy's in Plano. Let him hold it for collateral, get some money from him, get down here, and spring us."

I took a hard, deep breath. "No, man," I said. "No way! You got yourselves in, and you can get yourselves out. I'm gone." And before he could answer, I dropped the receiver back into its cradle.

Then I stood there staring at the phone until the realization of what I had done hit me. I had broken the cardinal rule: I had let the brothers down—left twenty-seven of them in jail, twenty-three card-carrying members of the third largest gang of outlaws-on-wheels in the nation, plus four of their mamas. I already knew the fury of these guys firsthand. Nothing short of blitzkrieg would keep them from blowing me away. They were crazy . . .

. . . like what happened in Fort Worth two months earlier just because of something one girl said.

Tank from the Fort Worth chapter and some of the Dallas guys and I had been sitting in our club house on Worth Street, telling stories and downing a few beers, when the girl came in. She flopped down on the big green over-stuffed chair and said, "The guys in Fort Worth say

I'm here and I ain't leaving!

the Bandidos don't know how to party." She was looking right at Tank.

Tank frowned at his beer can for a minute, then dragged his six-foot-seven hulk up off the couch.

"Who said?" he wanted to know.

"The Mescan club," she said. "You know, the one that has its own shop? I was just there. I heard them."

Tank walked to the fireplace and, with the studied precision that meant something was about to be destroyed, he lined his beer can up with about a dozen others along the edge of the mantel. He pulled up the front of his frayed, black tee shirt and scratched his bare belly, then said, "Let's show them how to party."

Seven of us piled into the van. We drove to Fort Worth and parked in front of the Mexicans' shop. When we walked in, two Mexicans were working on a torn-down bike in the back room, two others were standing near the wall, drinking beer and talking, and the fifth guy was seated behind the counter near the cash register, studying some papers. Tank sauntered over to the counter while the rest of us milled around, waiting to see what would happen.

Reaching over the counter, Tank took the papers from the guy's hands and said, "Where's your president?"

Without looking up, the Mexican said, "He's home."

Tank said, "Call him."

The guy looked up at Tank, then over at us. We all topped six feet. "What's it about?" he asked Tank.

"Call him." It was obvious that Tank didn't want to discuss it with him.

"Yeah, okay. Take it easy. I'll call him." The guy shifted around on his stool so he could keep his eyes on Tank while he dialed the phone. He said a few words into it in Spanish and hung up. Tank, dropping the papers on the counter, was getting agitated. If that presi-

Delivered

dent didn't show up fast, somebody could end up dead.

When he did show, he had two other guys with him. Without appearing to notice Tank, he said to the guy behind the counter, "All right, I'm here. This better be important."

The guy nodded his head towards Tank.

The president looked up. He seemed bored. "Well?"

"The word is out that the Bandidos don't know how to party."

"Man, what are you talking about?"

One of our guys, who was leaning against a four-drawer metal file cabinet, gave it a shove and sent it crashing to the floor. The two Mexicans from the back room dashed in, and we started swinging our chains. As a finale, Tank hoisted the frame of a Harley and crashed it through the plate-glass window. Six Mexicans were laid out and blood was everywhere. The other two split, and so did we. No cops would interfere because nobody would sign a complaint. It was over in less than three minutes, and the whole scene happened because of something one girl said.

That's the kind of people I had left in jail.

Eight beers, half a gallon of rose and five joints later, and I still could not get high. Dislodging a scrap of tobacco from between my teeth with a fingernail, I went to the bathroom to spit it in the sink and throw some water on my face. As I leaned forward, I cringed at what looked back at me from the mirror: 300-plus pounds of sweating flesh, matted beard, filthy hair clumped into a heavy horsetail by a leather strap mottled by grime and sweat, red hate-filled eyes. I pulled off my shirt: neck and chest, covered with red splotches. I smelled like a goat, probably worse, but I could no longer tell. And now, leaning over the sink, coughing and crying, I was afraid for my life.

I'm here and I ain't leaving!

Stanley!

I grabbed my shirt, dumped some of my stuff into two cartons and an old cardboard suitcase, shoved them into the back seat of my rusted gray Falcon, and fought my way through Saturday morning traffic to my brother Stanley's apartment in Garland. I climbed the cement steps to the second floor and pounded the door on the left.

"Stanley! Stanley!"

Stanley's wife Sue opened the door. Stanley stood behind her.

Stanley said, "Johnny Wade, what on earth are you yelling about, man? Come on in here."

"You gotta help me, Stanley!" I pushed my way past Sue and the kids. "Stanley," I said, "I've left them and I'm scared to death. Your apartment may be small, but I'm here and I ain't leaving!"

CHAPTER TWO

"My life ain't worth nothing!"

Is he yet alive? He is my brother.   1 Kings 20:32c

1953-1962: Lubbock, Syracuse, Altus OK

    "Quit talking crazy, Johnny," Stanley said, "and tell us what's going on."
    The same question had been nagging me all summer: What's going on? I was the son of a praying Primitive Baptist mother, who for years had been rattling the gates of heaven on behalf of her alcoholic husband and their five offspring. And I never really knew what was going on. In fact, I had never cared before. I had never before worried about my future, but I wasn't eager to die, especially at the hands of the Bandido brotherhood. How could I have cowed myself into such a corner? Underachiever, yeah. Not motivated to achieve, okay. But I wasn't brainless. I just had never resisted anything before, nothing except responsibility. I always knew somehow that I could do anything I wanted to do. I just never really wanted to do anything until I started riding the big bikes.
    In 1953, we lived in the Homeplace, a big, 4-bedroom, 2-bath, gray-frame house in the middle of the block in the middle of Lubbock. Every room had its own different but still ugly wallpaper; mine had cowboys. I was a middle child with two brothers and one sister older and one sister younger. My brother Stanley, who had five

Delivered

years on me, was my idol. His adventures and escapades fascinated me, like in the movies.

Mostly I was afraid to try them myself until, in 1953, when I was eleven and in fifth grade, one of the guys said, "I know how to get cigarettes."

"You do?"

"Yeah, it's easy!" It was easy. We stole them. Then we smoked them in the back bedroom of a deserted house. After that house burned down, we would sit on an old junked sofa behind our garage, and smoke there. One day, when we heard somebody coming, we tried to snuff out the butts inside the torn cushions, then we ran. That night, when our garage burned down, we figured we had burned the deserted house down, too.

Daddy was an artist, a painter, but Mama could not stand his mess in the house, so he finally dumped it all outside and burned it. From then on, he drove a truck for the Red Ball Transfer Company, and was either gone for months at a time, or home engrossed in some TV program.

Mama was usually nursing at the hospital or nursing at the neighbors. Nobody seemed to care what we kids were doing, so, along with all our other unsupervised activities, we kept on smoking.

While Daddy was on a run for Red Ball in Spokane, Washington, one of his lungs collapsed. The doctors said cancer, but, when Daddy got home, he advised the family in nonnegotiable terms that he was not going to any more doctors, not going to take any chemotherapy or radiation or medication, not going to have surgery—subject closed. But from then on, he was in constant pain. Whenever he was home, he'd drink and smoke and cough and curse the world and everything in it until he'd fall asleep in front of the television.

Daddy had once taken Stanley along on a 3-month

My life ain't worth nothing!

run for Red Ball to teach him to be a he-man. Stanley came back a boozer, fighter and womanizer. Part of their "fun" in MacArthur Park in downtown L. A. had been in identifying the homosexuals, beating them up, then throwing them bodily into the lake.

After that, Stanley always had money and cars, but he was often in trouble, often landing in jail for packing a gun. Our cousins were not allowed to play with him or go riding in his car, but he didn't seem to care.

The year after I was twelve, Stanley went to prison after he was caught stealing. Mama couldn't talk about it without crying, and Daddy didn't try. One night, the three of us drove the 600 miles from Lubbock to Sugarland, pulling into the prison parking lot a few minutes before ten in the morning. While we waited with about forty other visitors for the gate to open, I stared at the ten-foot high, chain-link fence which was topped by what looked like a gigantic, elongated slinky decorated every foot or so with eight-inch, double-bladed razor bows. I hated the gate. I hated the fence. I hated the guards because Stanley couldn't come home with us. I knew I could leave when Mama and Daddy left, but Stanley couldn't leave.

Finally, at precisely 10 o'clock, the guard in the gun tower made a phone call. The heavy iron gate creaked, shifted gears and rolled back, and we filed into the prison yard, and the gate clanged shut behind us. The guards herded us through a drab cement building into a long room, and down one side of a long, 2-foot-wide table with a 14-inch-high glass divider down the middle. The prisoners were then marched in on the other side, where they sat down opposite their visitors. Guards at each end of the room, holding shotguns with live shells, made sure that everybody did what they were supposed to do.

The only physical contact we were allowed with

Delivered

Stanley was to stand with our hands clasped behind our backs and kiss him over the divider. The last time I had seen him before this visit, he was winning trophies at Buddy Holly Dance Contests at the skating rink in Lubbock while Mama thought he was in school. But this time he wasn't dancing. Soon, we had to leave, and the gates slammed shut behind us, shutting us out, shutting Stanley in.

When school let out in the spring of '56, I was thirteen—a teenager, but in reality a withdrawn, sickly kid. I was so scrawny, the relatives were beginning to worry about me. But Daddy decided it was time to toughen me up, make a he-man out of me like he had Stanley in the only way he knew. So that time he took me on a 3-month run for Red Ball through Oregon and Washington states to introduce me to boozing, fighting and womanizing. But unlike Stanley, I didn't want to do those things. Somehow I knew it would hurt Mama. So instead, I sat in the truck or in the motels or in the warehouses, stuffing myself.

When I checked into seventh grade in the fall, I was pale, fat and slow, the Pillsbury dough boy puffing down the football field and slugging in last in the relays. Our relatives had always bragged on how much I looked like Stanley—slim, dark and handsome with smiling eyes—but now they stopped. And the guys at school let me know that nobody wants to hang out with the fat boy.

When the other guys started dating, I settled for dirty jokes, dirty magazines, and a dirty mouth. I decided to become a loner (that sounded better than loser); then I could do whatever I wanted to do.

When my marks fell from A's to below average, Mama said, "You can do better than that." But the school counselor put a name to it—underachiever. He convinced me that I wasn't motivated. The fat girls and the

My life ain't worth nothing!

ones who wore glasses let me copy their homework. I never got caught, so I never felt guilty.

Two years later, when I was 15, I started patronizing the bootleggers of Lubbock, the "wettest dry town in the state of Texas."

Stanley and I laughed together at the elections when both Baptists and bootleggers voted "dry." The Baptists vowed that they didn't want any drinking at all, and the bootleggers didn't want to be out of a job. Working together for a change, they kept Lubbock County dry and the price of beer up. And I could always find a buck for a quart of beer or two bucks for a half-pint of Ten High, Daddy's favorite brand.

One hot afternoon in the summer of '57, I was alone in our front yard crushing buttonwood balls into the dirt with my heels, when Stanley came strutting down the sidewalk like Elvis the King. He sprinted across the street and into the yard right up to me, and he hugged me hard. "Johnny Wade," he said with a big smile, "hey, man, I made parole. After spending my eighteenth and nineteenth and twentieth birthdays behind bars, I finally made parole. Tell me, what does a '56 Chevy look like?"

We laughed and hugged each other. He didn't call me Fatty like some of the guys did, just Johnny Wade. We were laughing and talking when Mama came out and led him into the house, and I followed them.

Our oldest brother and a sister, who were both hairdressers, suggested that Stanley might want to do that, too. When he went to check out the beauty school, there he was with 101 girls. So he signed up and started beauty school, using the girls to bootleg his homemade booze at the dances. To them it was a game; to him it was a living.

In the fall of '61, since the other guys in my graduating class were enrolling in Texas Tech University, I did, too. What I really wanted to do was play pool—become

Delivered

an expert, a pool shark. So, when classes were in session, I was in the Student Union from ten in the morning when it opened, until ten at night when it closed, shooting pool.

At the end of October, I got a letter from the school, a summons to the office of the dean. I went to see what he wanted.

Mr. Moffitt," the dean said, "I have here the attendance record for the past five weeks, and I see your attendance is not very good. Do you have anything you want to say about it?"

"No, sir."

"Where were you during class periods?"

"Shooting pool."

"Why do you want to be in school then?"

"I dunno. Right now, I'm not too interested."

"Well, what do you want to do about it?"

"I dunno."

"In that case, I don't see any reason for you to keep on, do you?"

"No, sir. I guess not."

"All right, then, take this drop notice around to all your teachers, get them to sign it, and bring it back to my office."

I said, "Okay." I collected my books, got the signatures, and turned the slip in to the dean's secretary. They didn't seem to care, so neither did I.

Instead of hanging around pool halls waiting to be drafted, I went to the Air Force recruiting center and signed up. When I got home, Mama, smelling like Pond's Cold Cream and humming a song about angels and their snowy white wings, was standing at the sink washing dishes. Sitting on a kitchen chair behind her and staring at her back, I said, "Mama, if I want to, I can go into the Air Force."

My life ain't worth nothing!

She stopped humming. Without turning around she said, "Do you want to?"

"Yeah, I guess so. I went to their center today and took their tests and made high scores, so I can get into their electronics courses." I wanted her to turn around, to say something special, but since she didn't, I said, "I signed up."

After awhile, she said, "When do you leave?"

"I'm supposed to go to Amarillo for a physical and I'm supposed to be there on the fifteenth of December."

She washed a plate, rinsed it, then carefully stood it up in the drainer, then a glass, then a bowl. I thought she wasn't going to say anything else until finally she said, "Is that what you want to do?"

I thought, *Mama, Mama, won't you turn around and sit down and look at me and talk to me? Tell me if I'm right or tell me if I'm wrong. Talk to me, Mama. Please, talk to me.* But I said, "Mama?"

"Yes?"

"I can't go to school, and I don't have a job, so I'm going to go."

"All right, Johnny Wade, if that's what you want to do."

For the next six weeks, nobody mentioned it to me. But early in the afternoon of the day before I had to leave, Mama sat down on a straight chair in the dining room and said, "Come here, Johnny Wade." She patted her leg and said, "Sit here a minute."

A silent protest rose up in my heart. *No, I can't do that. I'm 18 years old. I'm big and clumsy and awkward. I'm over six feet tall, and I already weigh almost 250 pounds. No, I can't sit on your lap; I'd hurt you, Mama, and I ain't never gonna hurt you, never.*

"Sit down, Baby." She patted her leg again.

My weary overworked Mama in her nurse's uniform,

Delivered

white stockings and white shoes, sitting on our hard, old, worn-out, oak chair, looked up at me with an expression I couldn't figure out. I sat down off balance, pushing hard on the floor with the balls of my feet to keep from putting all my weight on her, hoping she couldn't tell how tense and uncomfortable I was. She slipped her arms around my waist, leaned her head against my back, and held me on her lap for about ten minutes without saying a word. Then she let me go. Her eyes were red, but she didn't say anything about it, so neither did I.

From Amarillo, where I had to report, I was sent to Lackland Air Force Base in San Antonio. When I completed Basic Training, I was rewarded with one stripe and a bus ride to Upstate New York, where I was supposed to study Russian with the prospects of a second stripe, a promotion, and my choice of serving my country in either Greenland or Alaska or Pakistan, monitoring Russian pilots' conversations and interpreting them for our government.

But I didn't want to do that. I wasn't interested in what the Russian pilots were saying. And I didn't care that the government was interested. What interested me was catching a ride on Thursdays to the Canandaigua Race Track to bet on the trotters, and bar-hopping every other day in Syracuse.

I really wanted to leave. New York State was no place for a "good-ole-boy" from Texas, especially when we were snowed in for three days in April, and the first of those three days was Easter Sunday. (Easter Sunday is supposed to be hot!) I learned, however, that after you sign with Uncle Sam, you stay where he puts you until he says you can go. And you don't cut classes. Cutting classes is AWOL. But you can flunk out. So, after doing assignments for three months, it took three more months of not doing them for me to fail the course. No second

My life ain't worth nothing!

stripe, no promotion, but I did get to leave New York. I was transferred to Altus, Oklahoma, which was close to home, and from there I could take my new friends home to meet Stanley.

By the end of my second year in the Air Force, if there had been medals for drinking, I would have been a fruit-salad colonel. So, when the top sergeant called me into his office, I thought, *Uh oh, they caught me. I wonder what I've done.*

"Airman Moffitt," he said, "we have a transfer here for you."

"Where to, Sarge?"

"You're going to Puerto Rico."

CHAPTER THREE

"Monkey-rum can make ya blind."

Ye looked for much and, lo, it came to little. And when ye brought it home, I did blow upon it.
                                    Haggai 1:9

1962-1965: Puerto Rico, Lubbock

A thousand air miles from Florida we touched down at the Ramey SAC Base in the northwest corner of Puerto Rico, a hundred-mile stretch of paradise where top-heavy palms nod towards narrow crescents of bright sand, feathering the edges of rocky jungles surrounded by crystal blue water—paradise, with cesspools. Aguadilla, where the base was located, was one of the cesspools.

We were warned about Mandango and monkey-rum: Everybody that shops in Mandango gets syphilis, and monkey-rum can make you blind.

Since the local citizens preferred that the American heroes not be friendly with their daughters, most of the island was off limits. We were, consequently, handed a list of places that were officially "on limits." Nearby Crashboat Beach was on limits, so it would do for a start.

I was delivering my dental records to the proper office when it was announced that President John F. Kennedy had been shot in Dallas.

Leaves were canceled, the base was put on alert, and I needed a friend like every adolescent fat boy with acne who changes schools in the middle of the term. But no-

Delivered

body seemed eager to open up to me, and I didn't know how to break through their invisible walls. I was clumsy, and there was too much of me stuffed into the uniform to look like I had class.

I didn't know how to talk, so I decided I didn't care. What would I say, anyway? That my baby sister was beautiful and always the center of attention? That neither of my brothers was fat? That when the neighbors were sick, they called Mama instead of the doctor, and she never refused to go? That whenever Daddy was home, there was lots of company, but not for me? That I couldn't talk politics and I couldn't talk religion, and what I really wanted was for Mama to hold me on her lap again?

Nah! Tough it out, laugh and say, "Who wants a beer?" There is always somebody to go with you to scout out the nearest bar.

Paoli's Bar squatted on the edge of Crashboat Beach, looking like a twenty-foot-square brush pile. Every day Paoli announced that he was open for business by propping up his lopping shutters and opening the door out onto the cement dance floor next to the shed that covered his flashy nickelodeon. Hard dirt made a good enough floor for the bar and grill inside.

We got passes and headed for Crashboat. There we were greeted by the shrieks and hollers of a full-scale brawl inside Paoli's. As we bolted in that direction, a sailor yelled out the door, "The hookers are killing Garbage John!" Sailors, airmen and Ricans from every direction converged on the building and crammed inside. I shouldered my way into the midst of the melee—a hundred people yelling and cursing and swinging their arms.

I fell in with some big sailors who were picking up the girls inside and passing them from hand to hand,

Monkey-rum can make ya blind.

then dumping them outside in the sand, while from the blinking jukebox Trini Lopez sang that he would "like to be in America."

While all this was going on, one of the sailors inside grasped the two tall two-by-fours, which propped up the palm-frond roof, and started shaking. He yanked the poles loose, and the whole roof collapsed on the wild crowd.

Paoli was beside himself, wringing his hands and crying, "Who's going to pay? Who's going to pay?"

Soon Air Police and Puerto Rican cops swarmed over the place, and the people disappeared like roaches when the lights come on.

Garbage John had brought it all on himself. He had been patronizing the prostitutes, then roughing them up and stealing their money. Together the girls were taking their revenge on him with broken beer bottles. It took ninety-eight stitches to sew him back up.

"Who's going to pay for my shack?" wailed Paoli, grabbing at sleeves.

Nobody paid any attention to him, but in a few days the two-by-fours were back in place, the flimsy rafters were up and covered with fresh palm fronds, the dirt floor was swept, and Smokey Robinson was belting out his songs. Paoli was back in business, peddling beer and rum and rice and beans from behind his greasy counter.

"Chicken today!" he called out, grinning over his good fortune. "Fresh from the cockpits."

"What cockpits, Paoli?" I asked.

"Good cockfights last night in Aguadilla, señor," he said, but then his face crumpled with sadness. "Poor chickens! I fry the losers. One piece, ten cents. How many?"

I turned to the beautiful Rican standing at my shoulder and asked her, "You want chicken?"

Delivered

"Sí, Gordito," she answered with a smile. "My name Chickie."

"All right, Chickie. How much?"

"Five and two."

"No, I mean, how much chicken?"

"Oh," she laughed, "just one stringy piece, Fat One."

Chickie and I stood by the bar, chewing on the tough legs of a loser and grinning at each other. And for the next couple of months, when I wasn't working and she wasn't working, we strolled the island together, munching fried pies stuffed with goat meat, potatoes, onions and cheese, drinking beer, and watching the people—watching the other hookers doing their thing, and watching the first "queers" I ever saw parading in public in tight pants, with hair rollers, blood-red lips and fake eyelashes, doing their thing—whatever it was.

At the base, when it was announced officially that JFK was dead, we went through the motions of a memorial service, not only mourning our dead President, but also wondering if some nation—probably Cuba—would start throwing bombs our way.

Everyone at the base was tense. I tried to hide the loneliness, the fear, the misery, like Daddy hid his suffering, by drinking whatever I could find, as much as I could find, until the hurt was lost somewhere in the haze and the hangover.

A few days later in Aguadilla, I was standing alone on dry ground not six inches from a curtain of rain that barely splashed my boots. I stuck my hand past the almost invisible wall, and it got drenched. I pulled it back, dried it on my pants leg, then stuck it out again, and I thought about Stanley. I wondered if he had ever seen anything like it. I wanted to show it to him.

I'd say, Hey, Stanley, look at that. And he'd say, Yeah, Johnny Wade, how about that? And I'd say, Have you

Monkey-rum can make ya blind.

ever seen anything like that before? And he'd say, Never have. And I'd say, Look, I can stand here where it's not raining, and if my hands are dirty, I can stick them out like this and wash them and not even get my sleeves wet. And he'd say, Yeah, Johnny Wade, that's really something. I'm glad you showed me that. I've never seen anything like that before. And he'd laugh a little, and I'd say, Yeah, it's really something, ain't it? And he'd say, I'm proud of you for showing me that, Johnny Wade. Thanks. And I'd say, Yeah, sure. And I'd know he was telling me the truth, that he was proud, because Stanley never lied to me, and he always called me Johnny Wade, and he never teased me about being fat. Then he would hug my shoulders and let go and laugh a little more and do a dance step and say, Cool, man. And we'd laugh together, and he'd go on in the house, and I would follow him.

I stood in the road, looking at the rain. The dry place where I was standing reminded me of the Panhandle and the South Plains of West Texas where it's desert on the caprock—miles and miles of uninterrupted dry sandy clay, where nothing happens in the soil until somebody plants seeds and brings water to it. Then soon it becomes miles and miles of dark green cotton fields, as though the water had washed the death from the brown seeds and the dry ground, and brought life. And I wondered, fleetingly, if I was like that dead earth, and if somebody brought some seeds and planted them and watered them . . .

Nah, I thought, *that's really stupid! Here I am. I can do whatever I want to do, and as long as I get my job done and show up at the base when I'm supposed to, nobody cares. There ain't nothing more to it than that. This is life, right? Yeah.* And I went on down to Crashboat to shoot pool and gamble.

Delivered

I made a bet and got into a game with a feisty Rican. While I was leaning across the table to make a shot, for some cocky reason I baited him by saying off the top of my head, "Man, you may win this game, but you ain't gonna win the fight."

For a quiet moment, I calculated the shot. Then, whoosh! Blinding pain slammed into my head, and the next thing I knew, I was in a corner across the room with the seat of my pants hard up against the wall and blood streaming into my eyes.

Through a black-red, star-studded haze, I squinted at the Rican, who had connected the heavy end of his pool cue with my forehead just a thin line above my glasses, and was now coming at me with his knife. I grabbed a chair by the legs and held it up in front of me, trying to punch him away with it, but he kept on stabbing at me. He was trying to kill me, and I knew I was about to lose the contest. I was that far from becoming a "war casualty."

Forcing my eyes to focus, the last action I saw was that of the big bartender, an American World War II vet, who buck-jumped the bar and grabbed the guy. Poking his .38 revolver in the guy's ear, he said, "Come on, Rican. Let's you and me go out that door."

Four stitches and three days later, I was assigned to the Toro, cutting grass eight hours a day, five days a week, back and forth, up and down, chasing mongooses all over the base.

On Wednesday, when I was beginning to enjoy it, the back left wheel of the Toro hit a hole, dropped down and popped back out with just enough of a jerk to wrench my body sideways and back as fast as it takes to tell it. Something inside of me exploded. I fell backwards off that sulky flat on the ground, rolled to one side and hugged my middle, while the Toro ran into a tree. I couldn't breathe.

Monkey-rum can make ya blind.

At the base hospital, where the doctors diagnosed a sprained diaphragm, they wrapped my torso in Ace bandages. A couple of days later they unwrapped my body, removed the four stitches from my head, and assigned me to light duty on the long pier at Crashboat where our freighters unloaded the JP4 jet fuel. My job was to pump air through the submerged empty fuel lines with an air compressor, while the divers swam along the lines and repaired them where they found air bubbles.

Mostly, I sat and chain smoked, missing Chickie, while I watched the shorebirds and pelicans squawking and diving for their dinner, and wondered who was watching us from the other side of that rolling mass of water, and what they were planning to do.

One afternoon, a familiar little figure came running across the sand, long straight black hair flying with the wind, waving and shouting, "Gordito! Gordito!"

I stood up and waved, then ran to meet her, grabbed her up in my arms, and gave her a big hug.

"Chickie! Where in the world have you been?"

"Oh, Gordito," she said, "I move to San Juan, go work at Lucky Seven, but I need you help me, give me clothes."

"What kind of clothes, Chickie?"

"Your clothes, Gordito, to hang in closet. Very bad man—what you call pimp—he beat me, he break into my place and say I work for him. But he afraid of GI. If your clothes in my closet, he go away."

"Don't worry, girl. You'll get the clothes."

With one of my uniforms and some civvies in Chickie's closet, the pimp stayed away. Then, whenever I went to San Juan for a weekend, I had a friend and a place to crash.

Like the Friday night between pay days, when one of the guys said to me, "Man, I'm bored with this base and that everlasting pinochle game. Let's go to town."

Delivered

"I can't go," I said. "I ain't got the cash. I got forty cents."

"Well, I've got about thirty-five," he said, "so let's throw it together, pay the *publico* a quarter, and catch a ride to the waterfront."

"And what are we gonna do with fifty cents at the waterfront?"

"Man, I'm desperate enough to try monkey-rum."

"Are you crazy? That stuff'll make you blind."

"Since when did you start caring about what makes you blind?"

"Well," I said, "there ain't nothing else to do. Might as well do that."

The hack driver let us out in front of a shack in a trashed-out alley behind a bar. He garbled something in Spanish to a hunched female figure on the dark porch. She in turn muttered toward a darker doorway.

An old man moved out of the shadows, shuffled down the steps, then hugged the bottom post while he squinted at us through red-rimmed eyes, murmuring something we couldn't understand.

"Rum," I said. My voice was too loud.

"Two dollars American," he mumbled.

"You ain't getting no two dollars," I said. "Fifty cents."

We haggled to a compromise—a gallon of rum for our fifty cents, my Zippo lighter, and our promise to return his crusty jug. We carried the jug to the beach and settled under the pier for a party. The brew that could make you blind tasted like gasoline washed through a dirty oil filter.

The next thing I knew, I was face down at high noon on a park bench in San Juan, ninety-five miles west of the monkey-rum brew-master who had my Zippo. A Rican cop was poking me with his stick and saying, "Hey,

Monkey-rum can make ya blind.

American soldier, you don't sleep here. Get up! Get moving!"

When I finally found my way to the Lucky Seven, Chickie, perched on a bar stool, saw me through the mirror, whirled around and shrieked, "Gordito! Gordito!" She slid down from the stool, grabbed me by the arm, and drew me quickly into the back room. "You look terrible," she said, "but you are alive! Are you all right?"

I felt lousy, but then I always felt lousy. I said, "Yeah, I'm all right. What's going on?"

"You don't remember, Gordito? The sailors, they were killing you. I hide you all day, then you disappear. Hurry now, quick. Go back to the base."

"Nah, Chickie, I'll just go shower and sleep at your place."

"How you do that? There's no time."

"I'm not afraid of them, Chickie."

"No, you got to be back at the base!"

"Not till Sunday."

"Sí, Sunday. It's four o'clock, Sunday. All day Saturday you fight, then you disappear. You no remember?"

I checked my pockets, then I remembered.

"Chickie," I said, "I don't have a cent!"

"Here, Gordito, three dollar. You go?"

"Yeah, I go."

"You go now?"

"Okay, Chickie, and thanks."

Every jolt on the Greyhound bus ride back to the base was agony. I had bruises on both sides of my chest, my jaw and both wrists. My hands ached, and I had lost a day. At the base I asked about the other guy.

"He's in the stockade, probably forever."

"What happened?"

"The Air Police arrested him yesterday afternoon, racing down the officers' beach, dressed in his tennis shoes."

Delivered

"That's all?"

"That was all."

"Did anybody see him?"

"About five-hundred people."

"What's going to happen to him?"

"Sixty days, then he'll probably be sent back to the world."

"He ain't blind, is he?"

"He'd be better off blind. He flipped slam out of his mind."

What did I learn from that weekend? Nothing. I drank and fought my way through twenty-two more months until one evening on the base, during one of the horror movies that was intended to help us laugh and forget war and home, a notice was flashed across the screen.

"Airman Moffitt, report to the C.O."

In his office, the C.O. said, "Your brother-in-law died this morning. Do you want to go home?"

"Yeah, I want to go home."

"When is your discharge date?"

"Two months from now—December."

"We can arrange for an early discharge if you want it. Meanwhile, be ready to fly out of here in the morning."

"I'll be ready," I said, and I thought, *I'll be ready, man. My feet haven't been dry since I got here.*

On the morning hop to Dover, Delaware, I kept thinking about Chickie. There had been no chance to tell her I was leaving. She would eventually sell my clothes; after all, she had to make a living some way.

From Dover, I caught a hop to Birmingham, then a commercial flight back to Lubbock. It was great being home again. Everybody was glad to see me.

"Good to see ya, Johnny. How long has it been?"

Monkey-rum can make ya blind.

"Two years."
"Hey, Johnny, where ya been?"
"Puerto Rico."
"Puerto Rico? I hear it's beautiful down there."
"Yeah, it is."
"What are you going to do now?"
"I dunno."

Then we ran out of conversation. Everybody went back to what they were doing. The guys from my highschool class were coming home from the service or graduating from Tech, getting jobs and getting married. Mama, as usual, was nursing at the hospital or the neighbors. Daddy, as usual, was on a three-month run for Red Ball. Stanley had moved to Dallas.

Peter Fonda was playing in *"Easy Rider"* at the Lindsay Theater. I saw it four times. I studied it, then bought a 650-BSA Lightning from a guy who didn't realize I couldn't ride. He took my money, and handed me the title and keys. On the way home I came close to causing an accident, but somehow I got to the caliche pit, practiced riding it, mastered it, smoked some dope, popped some pills—started feeling good. Control of the bike felt like Power. I began enjoying the whole scene riding through the park, smoking a joint, everybody looking at me strutting on wheels. It was a rush; it felt good. I studied motorcycle magazines, learned about motors, learned how to strip down a bike. I traded the BSA for a Harley-74, and turned it into a "chopper" like Peter Fonda's in *"Easy Rider."*

And, since Stanley was in Dallas, I decided to go to Dallas.

CHAPTER FOUR

"Yeah, I wanta do that!"

Every way of a man is right in his own eyes, but the Lord pondereth the hearts.   Proverbs 21:2

1965-1966: Dallas

"Hey, Johnny Wade! Come on in, brother. Have a beer. Is that your motorcycle?"

"Yeah, that's my chopper. You still styling hair, Stanley?"

"That's right," Stanley said, putting his arm around my shoulders as he ushered me into his apartment. "Just look at them trophies, forty-eight of them. Sue's my model in competitions all the way across the country. Man, I'm going to be the best hair stylist that ever lived! Sue, come see who's here."

Sue, grinning, came through the kitchen door with two cans of beer. She held one out to me.

"Sue, you gonna have a baby?"

"Yeah, Johnny. How'd you guess? I'm going to have a baby. And when you get through with that beer, you're going to have a shower!"

We laughed, and I said, "You got room for me for awhile till I can get a job and get my own place?"

"Yeah, Johnny Wade," Stanley said, "we got room for you. You seen Joel yet? He sure has grown since you saw him in Lubbock. He's six now and thinks he's twelve. He's a good kid—my bonus when I married Sue.

Delivered

Yeah, and now we're going to have our own."

Sue lit a cigarette and said, "Johnny, you and Stanley, well, he ain't as big around as you and you're only what? Twenty-three? But you two still look enough alike to be twins—tall, dark and good-looking. But you need to get in a hot tub and soak and get that hair shaped, and put on some clean clothes. The ones you're wearing ought to be burned."

"They ain't that bad!"

"Yeah, they are that bad."

"Now, Susie," Stanley said, "don't get on him yet. He just got here."

We laughed and, when Joel came in, I hugged him, and we all laughed some more, and drank some more beer.

I took Joel riding on my bike. I took him to the pool hall and to the ball games and to the park. I bar-hopped with Stanley and Sue, watched TV, and worked on my bike. I'd work a job for a month or two, get some money and move out to my own place, then quit the job and move back in, work and move out, then back in again.

The only thing that made me feel really good was being on my scooter flying. There was pure ecstasy, straddling 1200cc of power, feet crossed on the handlebars, a cigarette like a blowtorch in one hand and a Coors in the other, cranking the throttle to 100 mph, lying back on the sissy bar, and just letting her roll.

One Saturday morning early in '66, I went riding alone, heading north on US 75. After about half an hour on the road, I spotted a guy in the ditch a short distance ahead of me standing by his motorcycle.

I pulled over next to him and said, "Hey, man, you got a problem?"

"Yeah," he said, "but I don't know what it is. The thing just won't run."

Yeah, I wanta do that!

"Mind if I take a look?"

"Help yourself," he said, cursing the bike. "Think you can fix it?" When he turned his head to spit on the ground, I noticed a big patch on the back of his jacket that showed a ghost floating through the spokes of a wheel. I could also tell he didn't have any clean-freak like Sue nagging him all the time about baths and dirty clothes.

"Look here," I said. "Your spark plugs are getting fire, and your distributor is getting fire. Must be the fuel system." I checked and found that the fuel lines were clean, but the fuel filter was clogged with paint.

I said, "Man, look at this. How did that stuff get in your gas tank?"

"I just had the thing painted, but I don't know how that could have happened," he said, then he spit again and cursed some more.

I said, "Looks like whoever painted the tank didn't get the cap on tight." And I started digging the paint clogging the filter.

The guy cursed the painter and said to me, "I'm on my way to the guy's shop right now. I'm meeting some guys there. Where are you heading? You wanta come?"

"Yeah," I said, "I wanta come."

"Think you can get this thing rolling?"

"I can try."

Five miles down the highway and into Plano, we cut our motors at Roy's Bike Shop next to a vacant lot crammed with bikers, each on his own custom-rebuilt Harley. My friend stormed into Roy's shop leaving me on the edge of the crowd. The bikers, laughing and talking, joking and cursing, and passing around joints, all wore the ghost-and-wheel patch on their backs.

One of them walked towards me, planted his big dusty boot on the seat of my bike, and yelled over the

Delivered

crowd, "This ain't a bad-looking scooter! Who's it belong to?"

Several of them stopped talking and turned to listen. I looked him square in the eye and said, "It's mine, and if you don't take your foot off, I'll break your leg." Then I thought, *Uh oh, now I'll probably have to fight six of them at one time.*

The guy froze glaring at me, then slowly took his foot down, and started moving around the bike to my side. I could feel the heat rising.

My new friend, slamming out of the shop, quickly sized up the situation. "What's going on out there?" he yelled.

The guy with the dirty boot stopped where he was and said over his shoulder, "Blue, you know this citizen?"

"Yeah, I know him."

The guy smirked. Blue wheeled over on a loaner bike of Roy's, then said to him, "Yeah, I know him." Then to me, "What's your name?"

"Whale."

"Yeah, this is Whale. He's riding with us. Come on, brothers, let's git it."

Fifteen bikers, adjusting Harley head-bands and helmets, a few of them with girls mounted behind them, fired their motors at the same time, getting ready to ride, and I was in the middle—right in the center of all that thunder, all that anticipation, all that rush—with all those guys watching my friend Blue to see which way he was going to go.

According to the legend across the horizontal rockers on their patches, the guys were the North Central Texas chapter of the Ghost Riders, an outlaw motorcycle gang. The guy I had helped by the side of the road was their president.

Yeah, I wanta do that!

"What do you guys do?" I asked over the roar.

"We party, man. We roll and drink and smoke dope and party and have us a good old time. We get our bucks by dealing dope in Lee Park or White Rock Lake or the high schools, wherever the market is open. And our mamas, man, they are into the oldest profession in the world. And since they're doing it anyway, well, we hang around so they don't get into any trouble. Like a family, everybody takes care of everybody else. You wanta do that?"

"Yeah, I wanta do that. That's how I want to spend the rest of my life. What do I have to do?"

"Prospect for thirty days—do whatever we tell you and ask no questions. If at the end of the thirty days you get one blackball for any reason or for no reason, you're out. If not, you're in. Okay?"

"Sounds good to me."

"Okay, man, the rules are simple. Loyalty to the club is number one. Inner-club discipline is okay, but we don't want no pigs disciplining us, so don't bring no disgrace on the colors. No mainlining. No addiction. Don't be caught with no rig. Keep your pistol in your boot at all times, and your liquor bills paid."

I hung around the Ghost Riders, watching them, copying them until it started feeling natural. Sometimes we would ride all day or just hang around town, then stay at either Grape Vine or White Rock Lake at night. Mostly, we partied.

Nobody blackballed me, so Catfish said, "Come on, Whale, we're going to get your 'originals' so you can wear your 'colors,' man. Let's go shopping."

We borrowed a car and went to town.

"Look at that," Catfish said, pointing toward the stores, "ain't that something! That merchant is having hisself a sidewalk sale! And, look there, Whale, on the end of that rack. Ain't that your jacket?"

Delivered

"Looks like it, don't it!"

Catfish circled the block, then as he slowed down, I jumped out of the car, grabbed the jacket off the rack, and jumped back in. We took off down the street, leaving the shopkeeper jumping and shouting and waving his arms in the air. No problem. There were no cops near the place, and citizens don't like to get involved.

We met with the other brothers in Lee Park and drove to Cliff's house in Euless, where Blue presented me with my Ghost Rider patch. As soon as I chopped the sleeves out of the new jacket, Cliff's wife sewed the patch on the back.

The colors, the club—that's what mattered. In the club I had charisma; I had authority. When I told the girls what to do, they did it. When I told the guys what to do, sometimes they did it. Blue was impressed with my loyalty and with my cool in certain situations, so he appointed me master-at-arms, second only to him. Me, the new guy, an officer over the other twenty guys!

It was hard to talk about it to Stanley and Sue. They didn't understand that I needed the club, that I needed the colors, and that I needed the high.

"Johnny, get cleaned up! Johnny, get a job! Johnny, settle down!" It felt like time to move out again.

"Blue," I said, "this chapter is growing, and living loose is a bad scene, just hanging around town or out at the lake, with the guys sleeping around and out in the grass. We need a house, a nice big house in town where we can be together, keep our stuff together, party when we need to party—a place to keep the mamas under control and available. Then we can call the brothers when we need them, like in case we need bail, ya know? You need the house as much as the rest of us. Mongrel is always rounding up girls, and we need a place to take them."

Yeah, I wanta do that!

"Okay," Blue said, "you convinced me. You and Catfish find us a house."

We checked the ads and went house-hunting, and found the house on Worth Street—twenty-two rooms furnished in the middle of a block of rooming houses. The owner was glad to rent to such nice construction workers.

Three-hundred dollars a month to cover rent and utilities divided by fourteen live-in guys averaged just a little more than twenty-one dollars apiece. No problem. We were dealing dope and using the girls, and in an emergency we could sell our blood to the Blood Bank. I insisted that we always pay the rent on time. We didn't need any hassle from a landlord hanging around.

The first project we tackled on moving day was nailing the Ghost Rider flag over the French doors between the living and dining rooms. Then we took the doors down and stood them in a corner.

Since Blue was in jail that day, I was in charge.

"Now, listen, brothers," I said, "we're going to fix this place up. You guys that plan to live here, don't just come in and dump your stuff. Choose your room and dump it there. The room upstairs over this one is mine; there are plenty more, so stay out of that one. And stay outta the back downstairs bedroom. That's gonna be the grease pit."

One of our girls said, "Whale, Sharon and I are taking these sheets to the laundry. You got any dirty clothes you want washed?"

"Baby, we don't have dirty clothes! Hey, you guys, get to work. This ain't gonna be no pig sty. We're going to make it into a home. And quit butting them butts on the carpet. You're going to burn the place down before our guests arrive."

"Who's coming?"

"Man, we're throwing a party for the Lords, and

Delivered

they're bringing the booze—a christening for our happy home."

"Hey, Whale, ain't this the 'lectric chair?"

"Ain't you guys never been to church? Them are pulpit chairs. Leave them next to the fireplace. Blue and me, we're going to sit there to preside over our flock, and keep you guys alive and outta jail."

"Hey, the Lords are here!"

"Hey, man, gimme five!"

"Hey, man, who's this you got with you?"

"This is Whale, Chuck. He's in charge. And Whale, treat this guy right. He's president of the Lords."

Chuck said, "Where's Blue?"

"Man, he can't stay out of jail! Come on, Chuck, you being president of the Lords, you can sit in one of them pulpit chairs."

Chuck sat down and said, "You're having more company tonight than just us, Whale."

"Who's that?"

"The Bandidos in Houston heard about the house, and they're coming over to check it out. Hey, they're here!"

A few minutes later, Don, the Bandidos' national president, came through the door with three of his lieutenants. Chuck waved him over, then stood up to give him his chair.

Don said, "Yeah, so this is your house, huh? The Ghost Riders got a house—the Spook House, right?"

"Yeah," I said, "the Spook House! Let's drink to the Spook House!"

We sat down, and rapped about the guys and the house. He was impressed—he thought it was a great party, well run, lots of good stuff, nobody getting killed, nobody disrespectful.

As a matter of fact, the party was crazy and getting

Yeah, I wanta do that!

crazier all the time. Then, I looked up and saw a young cop standing in the middle of the room staring as though he had walked into a different world. Everybody was so high and wild, nobody noticed him except me.

I got up and walked over to him, and I said, "Idiot, what are you doing in here?"

He said, "We got a call from one of your neighbors that you are making too much noise."

"Man," I said, "you can't walk into my house like this. You got to knock on my door."

"I banged on your door," he said, "but there was so much noise, nobody could hear me."

"Look here, officer," I said, "you know that just about ninety percent of these guys are holding (armed), and you come walking in through that door like that. It's a wonder you ain't been just plumb blown away. Come on out to the porch. Man, you can't just come walking into my house. It's against the law."

"Okay, okay," he said, looking around with pure disbelief written across his face.

Out on the porch I said, "Okay, officer, thanks. We'll hold it down." And he got in his squad car and left.

When I came back in, Don was smiling. "Okay, Whale," he said, "look. I represent the Bandidos, and we want a chapter in Dallas, and I'm impressed with what you got going here. The Fort Worth Ghost Riders have already become Bandidos. We've partied with them and with the Ghost Riders from here in Dallas for years. This is a good club. I'll just put it to you straight. We want this chapter to become Bandidos. No prospecting, just say the word."

The guys who were listening started swaying and chanting, "Yeah, yeah, yeah," while Don told me what the Bandidos had that the Ghost Riders didn't have. They had a newsletter mailed monthly from San Antonio with

Delivered

news from the different chapters. They had official membership cards. They kept an attorney on retainer. They had hundreds of members, organized, with chapters in Galveston, Austin, Houston, Corpus Christi, San Antonio, Beaumont, Fort Worth, Little Rock, Shreveport and Monterey, and connections in Nuevo Laredo. And they wanted us in Dallas.

There were weekend riders: real estate men, salesmen, machine operators, ambulance drivers, who went back to their jobs and wives and kids. And there were nomads: losers who failed at everything they ever tried except getting high and acting mean, who were into crazy rape and perversion, who lived on their bikes. The majority were a little bit of both.

While we were discussing the pros and cons, the drunker we got, the better we liked the idea.

Most of the Ghost Riders signed to join. Since Blue said no, Chuck became president of the new Bandido chapter, and I became his vice-president. The Spook House would pass to the Bandidos. There were no hard feelings—we would still party with the ones who declined, and that was the important thing.

Our Fort Worth sponsors ordered our colors, the Frito Bandito with the big sword, from the Fort Worth Flag Shop. While we were waiting for them and for our ID cards to come up from San Antonio, we ripped the Ghost Rider patches from the backs of our jackets, dropped them into a pile in the back yard, soaked them with booze, and set them on fire. Fingering our new belts made from old Harley-Davidson motorcycle chains, we watched the old patches burn.

We thought we were climbing.

CHAPTER FIVE

"This is getting out of hand!"

It is of the Lord's mercies that we are not consumed.
Lamentations 3:22

1966-1969: Nuevo Laredo, Dallas, Garland

"All right, listen, you guys: Chuck said, let everybody know we're going on a run to Mexico. We're going to Nuevo Laredo."

"So, what's happening in Nuevo Laredo, Whale?"

"I dunno, but we'll find out when we git there, won't we!"

The following week at the border bridge between Laredo and Nuevo Laredo, each of us tossed his two cents into the toll-gate bucket, then roared across into Mexico. As we were checking into Jake's Motel, I noticed that more chapter officers than usually showed up for a party together had come on this run. Chuck got a private room for the two of us, but right away we headed for the Corpus chapter's rooms. I had noticed at the bridge that their officers had two girls who looked like they should have been at home in bed hugging their teddy bears. But when we got to the rooms, the girls were not there. Something was going on that I didn't quite grasp. I decided to stay as high as possible, while at the same time observing and listening and learning.

While we were partying, a guy from the motel came

Delivered

in. He hung around for awhile, then cornered the Corpus president.

"Where are they?" he asked.

"Upstairs. They won't give you any trouble. They're totally wasted on heroin."

"How much?"

"You know how much."

"Okay, four-hundred for the two."

The guy from Corpus nodded and the motel man counted out four-hundred bucks in cash. Then he turned to me. "You got any girls for sale?"

"Not this time." But the next time we had girls.

Lee Park in Dallas, where the police watch for runaways and used to arrest flower children for fornication and smoking dope, is as big as a city block—a beautiful, grassy, landscaped slope down to Turtle Creek, surrounded by elegant, elevatored apartments with balconies, where straights sip martinis and complain about government and taxes, and don't have the slightest idea of what is going on right under their noses.

Runaway girls from all over the country make their way to Lee Park. For a lot of them the trail ends there and picks up again on the white-black slave market across the border.

"Hey, baby, you want a ride?"

We took the willing ones to the Spook House and, with their permission, shot them full of heroin and made puppets out of them. They would mount behind us, lean forward and hold on, and we'd take them on our motorcycles to Jake's Motel. We weren't out to get rich, just looking for a way to keep our bills paid. But, it was a strange feeling sometimes, when I would be riding alone, remembering those young faces, wondering what happened to them, wondering about Chickie.

Nah! Too much frustration, too much hurt in this

This is getting out of hand!

world to care. I determined not to care. This was progress. Things were getting better for me. I was 25-years old and for the first time in my life I had real friends. I had status. I had money. The market was always there. It was just my turn.

Smoke another joint. Pop another pill. Have another beer. Get high, man. Just concentrate on the matter at hand. That's all you can handle.

My buddy Catfish signed up with the Navy.

"Ain't that kinda rash, brother? I know you've been wanting out for some time, being married and all, but ain't that kinda rash, joining up with the Navy?"

"I been thinking about it for awhile, Whale, and after the way the guys worked over Mack when he wanted out, I figured I'd join the Navy and let Uncle Sam worry about the details."

"Man, I'm going to miss you."

"Well, this ain't my bag anymore. Time to do something besides ride. I'll be seeing ya, Whale."

"Yeah, see ya."

When he was gone, I looked around the living room. It was trashed out—papers, beer cans, butts, somebody's lunch, clothes left where they fell, all over the place. I crossed the street to the pay phone on the neighbors' porch, called Mama collect, and told her how much I liked my new job, and how well I was getting along. I wanted her to be happy, thinking God was answering her prayers.

The guys in the house fought all the time. If one of them fell asleep with a bag of dope in his hand, there was nothing to keep a brother from helping himself and smoking it up. There was nothing to keep one brother from helping himself to someone else's money, nothing to keep him from picking up a girl out of somebody else's bed in the middle of the night. Then there would be a

Delivered

fight. Once in awhile there was restitution—booze or a bag of pills or scooter parts or another woman—but first the fight.

Cops were almost always parked about two blocks away, waiting to hassle a Bandit about his inspection sticker, or his horn, or his lights, or his driver's license, or the age of the girl behind him on the motorcycle. Then they would search him. If they found his dope or his pistol, they would take him to jail. So, whenever we wanted to go out anywhere, we would first send a guy who was clean to find us a route free of cops. After a party, if the cops were out, everybody who had a hot bike or an underage girl or no inspection sticker would sleep overnight and the rest would leave their pistols. We had an arsenal.

And the mamas were getting nervous. Every time they went out of the house to go to town or just to sit on the porch, some nosey cop would ask them how old they were.

In 1969, when we had been in the house almost a year, Stanley and Sue came to see me.

Sue put her hand over her nose as she picked her way through the trash to the kitchen. "Johnny," she said, "how can you stand this place? It stinks!"

Stanley said, "Johnny Wade, you're smarter than this. These bums think that the worse they stink and the sexier they act, that's how tough they are. Man, you ain't tough just because you're dirty!"

"These are my friends."

"Man, you don't need friends like that. Get out of here, get a job and make something out of your life. This place is crazy!"

Stanley didn't need to tell me the place was crazy. I knew it. I hadn't slept well in weeks, and I was getting

This is getting out of hand!

paranoid always wondering who was going to break in next, the police or some other gang.

Then, on the night of the run to Galveston Beach, Tiger and Cowboy get hit by the crazy driver.

A few weeks after that accident and after Stanley and Sue's visit, I was in my upstairs room, watching TV and trying to keep high. The party downstairs was wild, when one of the guys down there pointed his pistol up and pulled the trigger. The bullet went whip! zing! right up through the floor of my room, missing my arm by inches, and lodging in the ceiling over my head.

"That's it!" I said aloud. "This is getting out of hand. Tomorrow I'm making arrangements to sleep somewhere else besides here." The next two days I sent Sharon and Kaye to Stone Place Mall to panhandle for loose change. The first day they brought me $200 and the second day $150, enough to pay the deposit and a month's rent for an apartment I found in Richardson.

I took my TV set, a big oil painting of blue sailboats painted especially for me by my friend Mary, and the rest of my things to the apartment, stored the Ghost Rider flag in the closet, stocked up on beer and wine, pulled the shades, closed the drapes, and slept for fourteen hours. When I woke up, I was ready to party.

A few weeks later, while we were gone on a run to Little Rock, the police entered the Spook House, confiscated all the firearms and cameras they could find, then padlocked the doors.

Cowboy phoned me at my apartment. "Whale, what'll I do? We been evicted and the cops took my Winchester 30-30."

"Go to the station and get it, man. It's your gun."

But two days later, the word was out, that if anybody else wanted to claim his stuff, he could plan to spend forty-eight hours in jail first.

Delivered

At that point Snake and I decided to spend a couple days in Laredo until the heat was off in Dallas. Since my bike was in the shop, we rode double on his. On the way back through Waco, he missed a turn on the off-ramp, and we took a spill and a long painful slide down the pavement. The asphalt burned through my leather jacket all the way through my shirt, took the skin off my right arm and shoulder, and ground gravel into my flesh. Since the local health clinics would only take care of our VD, gonorrhea and crabs, and I didn't know any doctors in Dallas, I poured whiskey on it, screamed and moaned and called myself names, and hoped that it would heal. It didn't. It got infected.

Through nightmares, I relived the accident to Tiger and Cowboy over and over—the car coming over the hill, the impact, the screaming—but I was the one who was being flung out into the field, and I would wake up to find myself moaning with pain, with my arm and shoulder burning like fire.

Why was I not the one on crutches, or the one whose leg was gone?

Why did the other guy flip out on monkey-rum, and not me?

What's going on?

I knew I could not continue as I was. Something had to give. I had to make a change. Then, when I impulsively hung up the phone when Crazy Willie was calling me from jail, I knew it had to change fast.

In 1965, I showed up at Stanley's door leaving my chopper out front, strutting, smoking a joint, feeling good.

This time I was coming to hide.

CHAPTER SIX

"I don't want to go out there."

The hail shall sweep away the refuge of lies, and the waters shall overflow the hiding place.
                                   Isaiah 28:17b,c

1969: Garland

"Stanley, I left twenty-seven of them in jail. When they get out and find me, they're going to kill me. Man, they are crazy."

"Calm down, Johnny Wade. Just calm down. I'm glad you left them. Where's your stuff?"

"Some of it's out in the car. My bike's at the apartment."

"Well, we're going to get rid of that bike, and we're going to burn these clothes. You got any money?"

"Eight bucks."

"You got debts?"

"Yeah, I got debts."

"Well, we'll help you take care of them. You go on in the bathroom and clean up, then we'll get rid of that motorcycle."

"Johnny," Sue said, "you better get in that tub and soak, or you'll never get rid of that infection."

In the bathroom I yanked at the leather strips woven through the heavy horsetail that hung nine inches down my back. I used my left hand only since my right arm was still stiff and sore. When I finally got the leather

Delivered

strips out, clumps of hair came with them. It had been more than six months since I wove them in. After the third shampoo, even though the water was still running dirty, I decided that enough was enough. I stepped out of the greasy tub, dried, and stuffed myself into a pair of Stanley's Levis, then shaved with his razor, leaving my face raw and bleeding. I was in bad shape. The infection had spread to my neck and chest.

While Stanley tried to shape up my hair, Sue went to clean the bathroom behind me, but she wouldn't touch my clothes. Stanley stuffed them into a brown paper sack and sent Joel with them to the dumpster at the far end of the parking lot.

"Come on," Stanley said, "let's go sell that motorcycle. You got the title?"

"I got it. But, Stanley, I don't want to go out there."

"Well, you're going. Get in the car."

He drove me to the apartment, then I followed him on the bike to the shop in Plano. Roy was locking up for the day.

"How much will you give me for my bike?" I asked him.

"I don't need it," he said.

"Yeah, but you might. It's a good scooter."

"I don't need it," he said, "but I've got three-hundred bucks in cash right now, so I'll give you three-hundred bucks cash."

"Come on, man," I said, "I just paid you that much to fix it. You know how much it's worth!"

"To me right now today it's worth three-hundred bucks. Take it or leave it."

"I don't want to mess with it," I said. "Give me the money."

He went back into the office, opened the safe, and counted out fifteen twenties, then he handed me the

I don't want to go out there.

money, and I turned over the title and keys. At least it was $300 better than nothing.

I unpacked my stuff in Joel's room, slid my pistol under my socks in the bottom drawer of his chest of drawers, stuffed the Ghost Rider flag into one of my boots and stuck them on the top shelf of his closet, then stood my sailboat painting against the wall behind his bed.

Joel was ten, just three years younger than I was the summer everything changed for me, the summer I gained well over 40 pounds in less than three months. Blond, strong, tall for his age, Joel was determined to become a professional football player and was already working towards it daily by jogging and working out with weights. Michelle, who was just starting to walk, spent her days in a child-care center, while Stanley and Sue were at work, and Joel was in school.

I took up residence on the sofa in their living room. I smoked and scratched and watched every television show from test pattern to test pattern to keep from having to think, all the while glancing over my shoulder and out the window to see if the Bandits were surrounding the house. Comedies, quiz shows, soaps were fine. Sunday morning programs posed a problem until I discovered *The Lutheran Hour*, a series of dramas in which somebody always "got saved," but at least nobody preached and no choir sang *"The Old Rugged Cross." The Lutheran Hour* never made me feel like I had been to church.

Mama had always said that we didn't "get saved," we "were saved." Trouble came either because we weren't saved, or because God, Who was a Good Father, was always punishing His children with trouble. I knew without a doubt that I was one or the other because, much as I hated trouble, I always seemed to have plenty of it.

Delivered

Every time I heard a motorcycle outside, my stomach knotted. When the phone rang, sweat ran down my back and chest. If a car drove through the parking lot or a car door slammed, cold chills ran down my spine. In the bathroom, as soon as I closed the door, I was afraid to come out.

But nothing on television ever scared me. That was make-believe, and I had been in on the real thing. I had been with the guys when they worked somebody over, and I had done it, too. But, as far as I knew, nobody had ever done to the Bandidos what I had done to them, left them in jail. They couldn't let me get away with it without setting a precedent.

During that time I talked a lot with Joel. I told him some of the things that happened to Stanley and me when we were about his age, and he talked to me about school and football and Stanley and Sue.

"How come you don't call Stanley 'Daddy'?" I asked him one day.

"'Cause he ain't my daddy," he replied.

"Yeah, but he takes care of you and Sue, and he takes the place of your daddy."

"He ain't my daddy," Joel insisted.

I dropped the subject.

Stanley wasn't Joel's daddy, but he sure was trying to act like mine. He kept saying to me, "Johnny Wade, quit running scared. Look, I ain't going to be around forever, you know. It ain't going to hurt you to get a black eye; it ain't going to hurt you to get your lip busted. It'll go away after awhile, just like getting a spanking. It'll quit hurting after awhile."

"Stanley, man," I kept answering, "you don't realize these guys are going to kill me. They ain't just playing."

Sue didn't understand either. I was a different person from the one she had known. My life was like a stunt

I don't want to go out there.

car, racing up a steep ramp to fly over the pit to the other side. But, every time I thought I got to the top of the ramp, the momentum would fail and I would drop straight down. I had become a cowering introvert, unable to force myself even to take the trash out to the dumpster. I was positive the Bandidos were out there, waiting to kill me.

Not only that, but my infection was getting worse. One night I filled the tub with warm water, slid into it up to my neck, and fell asleep. Four times during the night, the water got so cold it woke me up, and I had to add hot to it. By morning my body was like an enormous bleached prune. But the scabs had soaked soft, so I took my knife and began scraping. Then I poured whiskey over it and screamed and cursed myself till it cooled down. In a few months, everybody had it—big open sores—Stanley on his ankles, Michelle on her hands and feet, everywhere anybody got a scratch. The doctor said staph, and Sue was furious. She and Stanley began to fight.

Then, early one morning, when I was sound asleep on the couch, someone tugged at my collar. It was Stanley with Sue standing behind him. "Get up, Johnny. This is it," he said. "Wake up!"

"Stanley, man, you scared me half to death. What's the matter?"

"Johnny Wade, you're going to get up off your rear end, get out and get a job. You've been here six months, and Sue and I ain't gonna support you no longer. We've got five-hundred customers, and any one of them can find you a job. So, Monday is it—you're going to get up, get a job, and move into your own place. We're through putting up with you."

"Man, what time is it?"

"Never mind what time it is. It's five-thirty."

Delivered

Sue and Stanley were up early that day because they planned to work during the morning, then drive to San Antonio for the Texas Hairdressers Association competition. If Stanley won, he would represent Texas in the national competition. While they were gone, Michelle would stay with a neighbor, and Joel would stay home with me. Joel had asked to spend the night just past with a friend, but Stanley had said no.

When it got to be almost 7 o'clock, the time Joel always joined me to watch *"The Three Stooges"* on TV and he didn't come in, I went to get him out of bed. No Joel.

I hollered at Sue, "Where's Joel?"

She came to the door and said, "What do you mean, where's Joel?"

"He ain't in his room."

Sue checked his bedroom, then the bathroom, then the parking lot out back. Finally, she called Stanley who went to look for him at the pool.

When Stanley returned, he said, "Is he back yet?"

"No, he's not, Stan," Sue said. "Did you ask the kids if they know where he is?"

"There aren't many out there, but I'll go knock on some doors."

At nine o'clock, Stanley returned without Joel. He said, "Sue, you go on to the shop and work this morning. Cancel my appointments and I'll stay here. When he shows up, I'll call you. Don't worry; we'll find him."

At ten o'clock, Stanley phoned the police. Bandits or no Bandits, I borrowed Stanley's car and checked at the bowling alley, the pool hall and the skating rink. None of Joel's friends would admit to knowing where he was, so we kept looking.

Sue came home at noon. About fifteen minutes later, Joel came strolling up to the apartment surrounded by his friends. Stanley met him at the door.

I don't want to go out there.

His friends said, "What are you going to do to him, Mr. Moffitt?"

Without answering, Stanley said to Joel, "Go in the living room and talk to your mother. And when you get through, I want to talk to you in your room with the door closed."

Sue, weeping with relief, told Joel how much she loved him and how glad she was to see him. Then Stanley, standing in the doorway with a belt in his hand, said, "Now I want to show you how glad I am to see you." And he took Joel into the bedroom. It was the first time in the four years since Stanley married Sue that he whipped Joel for anything. Then he restricted him to the apartment for the time they would be away, and they left.

After awhile the phone rang and Joel answered. "No," I overheard him say, "my daddy said I can't come out. They were going to cancel their trip unless I got home before they had to leave. Yeah, he whipped me—my daddy whipped me with his belt."

CHAPTER SEVEN

"This ain't the place for you."

So is the kingdom of God, as if a man should cast seed into the ground. Mark 4:26

1969: Garland, Lake Charles LA, Las Vegas

Pinkerton was hiring. One of Stanley's customers said I could probably get a job with them that didn't require any skills. It was a good place to start since, as a night watchman, I could carry my pistol and I would be working in the dark.

I said, "I'll go talk to the guy."

They hired me. They put me to work the following day, and sent me to a hat factory. I wondered what the owners would think if they knew they had a paranoid ex-officer of the Bandidos in a police uniform guarding their property.

Every night at ten o'clock, I drove the old Falcon through the gate, then chained and padlocked it behind me, parked the car somewhere inside the barbed-wire-topped, eight-foot fence, rolled up the windows, locked the four doors, and laid the loaded pistol on the seat next to me. Then, with the radio on full blast, I stared out the windows all night while waves of fear rolled over me hour after hour. After two months, when I began to relax hoping that the Bandidos had forgotten me, I heard the tail-end of a news report on the radio about some Bandits in Houston. On the way home, I ducked into a

Delivered

newsstand for a copy of the *"Dallas Morning News,"* and found a whole-age article with pictures of Little Lee, the president of the Beaumont chapter, and one of the guys in his club. They had rolled a guy in a Houston bar and killed him. Everybody knew Bandidos did it because they had been wearing their colors. The police chief began arresting Bandits, and it looked like he was going to arrest them all. But some of the other Bandits found Little Lee, worked him over, then dumped him on the floor of the police station with the promise that they would soon deliver the other guy. They didn't have to. He turned himself in to the police that afternoon.

The photograph of Little Lee made my stomach turn, and I decided it was long past time for me to go visit my Grandfather Corley, who was in the hospital far away in Glen Rose.

Oscar Corley was the gentlest man I ever knew. When I was a little boy he used to take me fishing at the river and tell me stories about Jesus and Abraham and God. Even though the stories didn't mean anything to me then, I loved listening to him because I knew he believed what he was saying.

When I got to the hospital, Oscar wanted to talk. He said, "Johnny Wade, during the Depression, when your mama was about eleven years old, I was out in Limestone County in East Texas with my mule, plowing up some dry bottom land. I hadn't made my crop that year because of the drought, and I was talking to the Lord about it. I was asking Him what good was I doing out there in the fields, when I wasn't getting any food for my family. Then I stopped in the middle of that field and prayed that God would show me the way."

Oscar's voice faded. He hesitated, like he was listening to something. Then, suddenly, in a clear strong voice, he said, "Johnny, right then in broad daylight, I

This ain't the place for you.

saw a shooting star. I saw it with my own eyes. It arched over my head and fell to the west, and I knew it was God leading me just like he led Abraham."

He paused again, then said, "I left that mule standing in the middle of the field, went back to the house, got my family together, and we followed that star all the way up the caprock till we run out of gas at the front steps of the Primitive Baptist Church in Tahoka. It was Saturday. When a man came to clean the church for the Sunday service, he found me and my wife and our young'uns on his front steps. He asked me what we were doing there, and I told him. He gave us a place to stay, and he gave me a job. Pretty soon, I had us a nice farm and some good land. We stayed there until your grandmother had a stroke, then we sold out and bought us some land here in Glen Rose by the river."

He stopped and chuckled again. "Never did find out who got my mule."

When Oscar talked about Abraham's following God, I didn't understand what he meant, but I saw that Oscar Corley was experiencing something I didn't know anything about. He was dying, and he had peace. And without my knowledge or understanding, he was planting a seed in dry ground.

I went back to Dallas, back to my job with Pinkerton, back to television all day and radio all night.

Late one morning on my day off, the telephone rang. I was groggy when I answered.

"Yeah?"

"Whale, is that you?"

My heart leaped to my throat. Nobody called me Whale except the Bandits. What should I do? If I hung up, he'd know it was me. If I didn't hang up... The only thing to do was tough it out.

"Yeah? Whaddaya want?"

Delivered

"Whale, this is Cliff. I want to come out and see ya."

I swallowed hard. "What for?"

"The flag, man. The Ghost Rider Flag. Have you got it?"

"Yeah, I got it."

"Okay," he said, "I'll come out and get it."

"How do you know where I am?"

"Man, that ain't no secret." And he hung up.

I spent the rest of the morning stewing, wondering if I could trust Cliff, watching the road from the window in Stanley and Sue's bedroom. Somehow I missed seeing Cliff drive in. When he knocked on the door, I almost jumped out of my clogs. My hands were shaking.

Man, I thought, *this is ridiculous. If he's going to kill me, he's going to kill me.*

I opened the door and there was Cliff with his wife. I relaxed. No biker is going to kill somebody with his own wife standing there watching him do it.

They came in, and I said, "Wait here. I'll get the flag."

I went into Joel's room, wiped the sweat off my face, and retrieved the rumpled flag from my boot, then took it to Cliff.

I said, "Cliff, I want to ask you something. How come the Bandits haven't tried to get even with me?"

"Man," he said, "somebody must be watching over you. They were going to waste you good. The nomads were screaming for blood, but me and Mongrel and Lucky, we knew you had been wanting out for some time; we told them to blow it off, that you weren't going to tell nobody nothing. Crazy Willie was furious. Man, he ain't a good one to have for an enemy. He thinks anybody that is not a Bandido is expendable. Anyway, we argued about it for three or four hours, and after awhile everybody cooled off."

This ain't the place for you.

"What about Little Lee? You know about him?" I asked.

"Yeah, I know about him."

"Who messed him up?"

"The president got Crazy Willie and Apple to do it. He decided that it wasn't too cool that the police were arresting Bandidos. That idiot Lee, he told them cops that, when he got out of prison, he hoped the Bandidos would take him back. You know, Whale, the Bandits didn't whip him like that because he killed that guy, but because he had his colors on when he did it."

"Yeah, I know: 'Don't bring no heat down on the club.'"

"Yeah. Well, thanks for the flag. We'll be leaving."

"Yeah, take it easy."

Cliff's visit shook me up. If he could find me that easily, it was time to get way out of town. Maybe the Bandits had cooled off, but maybe they hadn't.

That night at a bar I got to talking to a guy who had just been hired by the Texas Electronic Security Systems, Inc. (TESSI), to install burglar devices in Lake Charles, Louisiana.

"They're still hiring," he said, "and you might get better money for your time. Why don't you go down and apply?"

"Yeah," I said, "I might do that." There were no Bandidos in Lake Charles.

The man in the TESSI office never ran a check on me. He just asked me what I was doing then, and I told him I was in the security business.

"That's great," he said. "What do you know about electronics?"

"Nothing."

"Well, we can teach you."

Delivered

I resigned from Pinkerton, who gave me a written recommendation, and I moved to Lake Charles.

In late November, I got a call that Mama was in the hospital in Lubbock with terminal cancer. My boss said, "Catch the next plane. We'll keep you on the payroll."

The day after I arrived, Mama slipped into a coma. I knew she had faith, and I found myself believing that, when she died, she would go to be with Jesus. I didn't exactly know who He was, but I knew that He had been her life.

I sat in her room, remembering the time she held me like a baby on her lap just before I went into the service. I remembered all the times she planned to do something for herself. But, a neighbor would call to say that somebody was sick, and she would barely hesitate before saying, "I'll come."

I looked at her lying there in the hospital bed, and I thought, *She must be like Jesus was.*

At eleven o'clock, the nurse said to the doctor, "Mrs. Moffitt seems to want more pain medication, but she's had all she can tolerate."

The doctor examined Mama, then with tears in his eyes he said to the nurse, "Give it to her." And at one o'clock in the morning, she passed quietly away.

The doctor and the nursing nuns, who saw this every day, were weeping for my mama, who had worked alongside them for so many years; they were weeping with me. In my heart I asked Mama to forgive me for being selfish and hating the neighbors for taking her away from me. They couldn't help being sick.

"Mama," I said between sobs, "are you happy now?"

Daddy wanted me to quit my job with TESSI and stay in Lubbock. If I would live with him, he said, he would pay my way through business college. But I didn't want to do that.

This ain't the place for you.

I went back to Lake Charles, but soon TESSI came on hard times. Just before they folded, they gave me a letter of recommendation. Then I had two, one from Pinkerton and one from them. I was almost straight—drunk most of the time, but almost straight.

Back in Dallas, I struck up a conversation with two guys in my favorite bar. We planned how we would burglarize the warehouse of a coin-operated candy and cigarette machine company where I had installed a burglar alarm system. The place was piled high with sacks of quarters, and I had figured out how to get in. The men were so eager, they could almost taste the money; they could hardly wait to make the score. I described in detail how it could be done, and told them everything except the name of the company and where it was located.

Then Stanley came back from a hairdressers competition in Nevada and said, "I met an old friend of yours in Vegas, Johnny Wade, a buddy from the service. He wants you to get in touch with him."

I phoned my friend who said, "Johnny, if you ain't doing nothing special you need to get on up here to Vegas. There's gambling and drinking and women and jobs all over the place. This is the land of opportunity. This is the best place I've ever been."

It sounded just like what I was looking for, so I hocked what I could and, without giving another thought to the guys waiting at the bar, I drove to Vegas, arriving at my friend's house broke, out of gas, and thirsty. At their insistence I halfheartedly looked for a job, but mostly I wanted to watch TV and drink to old times. After a few days, his wife was talking divorce.

Finally, the guy said, "Look, Johnny, I was wrong. This ain't the place for you. Take my credit card, get your gas or whatever you need, and go on back home. When you get to Lubbock or Dallas or wherever you're going,

Delivered

just mail the card back to me. Why don't you just go on back tonight?"

As I reached for the card, I felt like the whole world was a tuxedo, and I was a pair of old brown shoes. I went home to Daddy.

"Well," I said, "you win. I'm ready to go to business school."

CHAPTER EIGHT

"Church? What's her name?"

Purge me with hyssop, and I shall be clean. Wash me, and I shall be whiter than snow.   Psalm 51:7

1970-1971: Lubbock

After us kids had left home, but while Mama was alive, Daddy divided the Homeplace through the middle, built a kitchenette where the back bedroom used to be, and rented out the back half. Consequently, after I moved into the front half with him, I stacked my pornography in what used to be Mama and Daddy's bedroom, and he stacked his in what used to be the family dining room. We guzzled beer like it was a contest.

Well, I thought, *at least this arrangement is better than prison. If we had pulled off that burglary in Dallas, I could have gone straight to the pen.*

Daddy delivered the *Lubbock Avalanche Journal* seven days a week on a two-hundred-mile circuit of main drop-off points west of Lubbock. He loaded his truck at the newspaper office at one o'clock in the morning, and got home six hours later.

I enrolled in Draughan's Business College, a severe looking red-brick building on a treeless property in the middle of Lubbock. I got a bank loan to cover books and tuition, then applied for veterans' benefits that would give me $260 a month for living expenses. I also drove

Delivered

the route for Daddy a couple times a week to give him some time off and put a little extra cash in my pocket.

Draughan's Business College was a strange place for me to be at the time. I was twenty-six years old. I had graduated from high school the same year the other students entered fourth grade.

I was also letting my hair grow long again, still smoking dope, and still carrying my pistol in my boot—never out of the house without it. I figured the main thing for me to do was to beat these young students out of their money in a floating poker game during breaks to support my $20-a-day beer habit.

Meanwhile, my old friend Boxi, who had stepped on a land mine in Vietnam and blown off his right foot, came back home to Lubbock by way of the Amputees' Hospital for War Veterans in El Paso. He and I were the only singles left in the old gang. He had a plastic leg, a substantial monetary arrangement with the Military Retirement Insurance program, the managership of a local liquor store, and a new Corvette. He was looking for a house.

Daddy had become as bad as Sue about my changing the sheets on my bed, so, when Boxi bought a big shambles at the gravel-pit end of Buffalo Springs Lake in Yellow House Canyon just outside of town, the three of us agreed that I should move in with him.

Boxi and I decided to remodel the old house. First, we put out rat traps and roach traps. Then we set up his water bed. Then we announced to our friends that anybody who wanted to come out and work was welcome.

For starters we dismantled the wooden wall niche for the hall telephone and rebuilt it into the living room wall six inches above the floor as a station for Boxi's jade-green, plastic Buddha. We painted the niche black and hung black iron candle holders on each side, then threw

Church? What's her name?

a pillow down in front of it. We painted the rest of the living-room woodwork black, then covered the lower half of the walls with charcoal-brown paneling and the upper half with navy-blue burlap. The furniture was limited to a couple dozen pillows, a single-bed mattress covered with orange fake fur, and a white porcelain commode. The only light came from the knobs on the stereo.

In the dining room we covered three walls with rust burlap and the fourth wall behind the wet bar with bright orange velvet on which we hung a huge mirror and some glass shelves. On the opposite wall and reflected in the mirror was a five-by-two-and-a-half-foot abstract of a Playboy centerfold, also painted by my friend Mary, in shades of red with black shadows. There was one fluorescent light under the counter and a twenty-five-watt bulb in a blue-glass, Spanish wall fixture.

Our friends and their wives came often to work and stayed to party with us far into the night. Our trash and garbage got pitched together out the kitchen window into our private landfill project, where the rats had an ongoing party of their own.

Meanwhile, at Draughan's, where I was teaching the kids how to play Tonk and stealing their money, a pretty girl named Kathleen often came and sat next to me at the table. She showed no interest in the game, never learned how to play, just sat there making me nervous. She was like no girl I had ever known, nothing like the girls at the Spook House or the bargirls or the cowgirls I knew—more like Mama. She was always groomed like she had just graduated from charm school. I started taking showers every day.

Finally, one day I said to her, "Would you like to go out with me, darlin'?"

She almost jumped off the side of her chair. "No!" she yelled.

Delivered

"Well, okay," I said. "You don't have to pitch a hissy."

Now she really had me puzzled. What did she want? I knew my cursing bothered her, but she never mentioned it. I didn't know how to talk without cursing. That was my vocabulary. Daddy cursed, and I cursed; I couldn't help it. We played cards, and I raked in the money and told dirty stories and cursed, and Kathleen sat there and smiled, like she was perfectly content, like she knew something I didn't know. I couldn't understand it.

I asked her again. "Do you want to go somewhere with me?"

"Nooo!"

The next day, she would be sitting there again, and I would ask again.

Same thing. "Nooo!"

Finally, one day after Christmas break she asked me if I would go to church with her.

"You bet!" I said. "I've been trying to get a date with you for weeks."

It didn't make any difference to me where we went. Churches didn't scare me. My experience with church was going with Mama once a month to a short service followed by a big picnic. There certainly wasn't anything spiritual about that. Preachers didn't spook me at all. They were just good con men trying to make a living, telling lies and taking offerings so they could drive around in their big cars. Nothing spiritual about church.

Boxi said, "What are you getting all cleaned up for?"

"I'm going to church."

"Church? What's her name?"

"Kathleen."

When I went to pick up Kathleen, her mother and father came, too. That was a new twist, but it was a start.

The Trinity Church sanctuary, a large modern room

Church? What's her name?

shaped like a circus tent, had ceiling rafters pointing towards a center skylight that the members laughingly called the glory hole. A visiting minister told them that, when Jesus comes in the sky, they would all be sucked up through the glory hole to meet Him in the air. When Kathleen told me that, I thought they were all crazy.

Rows of pews fanned out in front of the stage. On the wall behind the pulpit hung a plain, wooden cross about eight-feet tall. But what disturbed me about the church was that the people were happy.

Nah, I thought, *people ain't happy. They just talk about being happy.* But one thing about these people, they were all smiling, and they sure did look happy.

A man in a sharp business suit—at least a $300 suit—came over to me and threw his arms around me in a bear hug. He smiled right into my face and said, "We sure do love you, and we're glad you're here this morning."

"Man," I said, "you better back up and cut me loose."

But he kept on smiling. I had long hair, bloodshot eyes, pot in my pocket and a pistol in my boot, and the guy kept smiling at me like he really did love me. It was unreal.

"Who's the guy?" I whispered to Kathleen.

"LeRoy Deardorff," she whispered back. "He's one of the elders here."

"Well," I said, "he's stupid! He's a nut!"

But, if he was the one who was stupid, why was I the one who was feeling stupid? It didn't make sense, and I didn't believe him.

As I looked around, I saw something else that didn't make sense. Kids from town who I knew were dope pushers, addicts, prostitutes and thieves, some of them barefoot, were sitting together with open Bibles, listening to the preacher preaching about Jesus as though he

Delivered

knew Him personally. Next to me was a girl with no shoes on her feet. Next to her was the man in the $300 suit. Street kids, straight kids, business people, farmers, rich folks, poor folks, Mexicans and me, and I was there just to see if I could make out with this girl who had been bugging me. I decided to listen to the preacher, so I forced my attention away from the people and concentrated on his words. What he was saying was so far-out, that for awhile I forgot about Kathleen.

When the meeting was over, I needed an excuse to come back to this crazy place, so I said to her, "Do you want to come back here with me again?"

"Sure."

"When can we come back?"

"Tonight?"

"Yeah, tonight. We'll come back tonight."

Kathleen told me the street kids with the bare feet were there at the church as a result of a revival crusade the month before led by a young traveling evangelist—all those kids in the raveled Levis with long hair straggling down over their shoulders, with the double-knit church people there loving them.

At the end of a wing off the sanctuary was the Living Room where counselors were available around the clock to share from the Bible and counsel and pray. I started hanging around there in my spare time, listening to them talk about Somebody who actually let His enemies hammer big, rough spikes through His hands and feet—for my sake!

Finally, I said to one of the counselors, "Tell me how to get to heaven without saying I have to 'get saved.'" I had decided that Mama was right. The term "get saved" was ridiculous. She knew she was a child of God, and she never "got saved." She knew her daddy didn't "get

Church? What's her name?

saved": he "was saved" on the steps of the Primitive Baptist Church in Tahoka.

"Tell me how I can get to heaven, but don't tell me I have to 'get saved.'"

I didn't understand the answer, but for about two months with or without Kathleen I was in church every Sunday morning, every Sunday evening, and every Wednesday night. In between times I hung around the Living Room, watching and listening. Something kept drawing me back.

On the last Sunday in March, Garry Page, the newly hired youth pastor, was scheduled to preach his first sermon for the entire congregation during the evening service. That same morning right after the service, Kathleen began to cry.

"My goodness, girl," I said, "what's the matter with you?"

"You're just sorry!" she said. "I'm through wasting my time with you. I give up. I've had it. You've had plenty of time to get saved, and you'll never do it. From now on, you can count me out!"

I drove her home in silence, then I said, "I agreed to take your parents to church tonight, so you're just going to have to put up with me one more time."

That evening, when Garry began to preach, I looked up at the skylight and pictured the whole congregation floating up through the glory hole, leaving me sitting on a pew.

Garry preached from the first half of the fifth chapter of 2nd Kings in the Old Testament, about the healing of Naaman the Syrian. He said, "God has done everything He is going to do for you. He gave His Son to die on the cross that you might be saved. Now it's your turn to do something about it." (Garry may have been teaching about Naaman, but he was talking about Johnny.)

Delivered

"You can sit there as filthy as you are for as long as you want," he said, "or you can get up and go wash. It's nobody's decision but your own."

I was stunned. Suddenly, my hair felt two-feet long, and the pistol in my boot was chafing my foot. I couldn't even remember if I had taken a shower before church. I looked up at the skylight again and felt panic. I knew I had to do something, but I didn't know what.

"You can sit there and be filthy, or you can go wash."

Garry bowed his head to pray. Then, as Pastor Morris Sheats walked down the steps from the platform, and the choir began to sing, Garry looked up and spoke into the mike, "If anybody wants to get saved, the pastor ..."

As clear as a bell over the voices of the choir, I could hear Mama singing through the glory hole:

"O come angel band, come and 'round me stand.

"O bear me away on your snowy wings to my immortal home.

"O bear me away on your snowy wings to my immortal home.

"My latest sun is sinking fast (I was her latest son!)

"My race is nearly run ..."

I cried out, "Mama!" and I came up out of my seat and started running down the aisle. The further I went the faster I got, and the more it was apparent that all 300-plus pounds of me was not going to be able to stop.

Pastor Sheats, who was standing in front of the pulpit waiting for the people, saw me coming just as I grabbed him by the head and spun him around. I was bawling like a baby. When he finally caught his breath and calmed me down a little, he sent me with two counselors to the prayer room where we knelt together, and they began to pray.

One of them put his arm around my shaking shoul-

Church? What's her name?

ders and said lovingly into my ear, "Brother, what do you want from God tonight?"

"I wanta go waaaash!"

"Brother, do you want everything God has for you?"

"Yes, everything!" I sobbed and sniffed and choked and bawled.

The men started praying for me in words I could not understand. Then I started praying in words I could not understand. I thought I was just blubbering, but it was real: It was the gift of tongues, the Holy Ghost praying through me supernaturally for God's will.

I had gone into the prayer room filthy. Five minutes later I was clean: saved, committed to Jesus Christ and praying in a supernatural prayer language straight to the heart of God.

What's going on? I wondered.

During the weeks I had been going to the church, I had heard a lot about the Father, the Son and the Holy Ghost. The Father was God—no problem there. The Son, Jesus. That's all I had heard since I'd been coming. But, the Holy Ghost? I figured it out. Jesus was holy. And, after they killed him, He rose from the dead. Dead people walking around are ghosts, right? So, Jesus after His resurrection walking around on the earth for forty days—the Holy Ghost! Simple!

"No, Johnny," one of the counselors said. "Let me show you in the Bible. The Holy Ghost is not a spook; He's God."

"Johnny," the other counselor said, "I don't know anything about your life, but the Lord is impressing me to share a verse with you. It's Luke, chapter 1, verse 74. Listen to this: 'That He would grant unto us that we, being delivered from the hands of our enemies, might serve Him without fear.' Does that mean anything special to you?"

Delivered

"Yeah, that means something special to me." It meant that I could serve God without fear of the Bandits, that's what it meant. That one verse from the Bible demolished the terror that had controlled me.

I left the prayer room and went into the darkened sanctuary, where Kathleen was waiting for me to take her home. Her parents had already left.

"What happened?"

"I got saved." The peace I was feeling was incredible.

She started grinning.

"And I got baptized in the Holy Ghost."

Her grin got bigger.

"And, you know what?"

"What?"

"I think—no, I know that I'm going to work for Jesus."

Her face crumpled, and she started crying again.

"Girl," I said, "what's the matter with you? This morning you were bawling because you thought I'd never get saved. Now you're bawling because I did."

We laughed, and through her tears she said, "Johnny, it's wonderful. It's a miracle."

When we drove up in front of her house, I said, "Kathleen, before you go in there's something I want to tell you. When I was with the Bandidos, one day when we were in Lee Park, some Jesus freaks were passing out tracts and sitting around on the grass singing. One of them came up to me and said, 'Do you know Jesus?' And I said, 'Yeah, man, I know Jesus. He's in the Dallas chapter.' I thought he was asking about a biker from Richardson, who wore his hair and beard like the Jesus in the pictures. My answer blew the kid's mind, so I said, 'Well, why did you ask me if you didn't think I knew him?' Kathleen, that's who I thought the guy meant—until now."

Kathleen laughed and cried some more, and I said,

Church? What's her name?

"Remember all the times I kept telling you, like I knew what I was saying, that it doesn't make any difference what you believe as long as you're sincere? Well, thanks for not turning me off, for not letting me convince myself. Thanks for praying. But, how could you stand it so long?"

"It wasn't easy," she admitted. "You really used to scare me, the way you looked, and the way you talked. I would just cringe. But I knew God wanted to save you, so I kept praying. He gave me the strength and courage to keep after you."

Kathleen went into her house, and I went home to the lake, kicked my way through the dark and the trash to my room. I went to bed.

When I woke up the next morning I thought, *What happened? How come I ain't sick?* I had no hangover, no withdrawal, no desire for booze or dope or pills. I wasn't tempted to take the latest girlie magazine with me into the bathroom. As a matter of fact, I didn't want to touch it. I wanted to read the Bible. I even thought about Kathleen differently, saw her with different eyes. She was beautiful, my sister, a faithful friend.

The following Sunday evening, I was baptized in water at the church. Just before Pastor Sheats put me under, he asked me to give a thirty-second testimony about what God had done for me.

In thirty-five seconds I told how, through pure rebellion in my heart, I had been a leader in one of the worst gangs in America, but that Jesus had found me, saved me, and filled me with joy. I was bawling again, and when the Christians stood up to praise God, it sent chills up and down my spine.

When we were changing back to dry clothes, Morris shocked me by saying, "Johnny, I want you to give your testimony on my TV show."

Delivered

"Well, I don't know, Pastor," I said. "I'll have to talk it over with my dad. This is his town, and some of the things I would say might not make him too happy."

"Okay," Morris said, "that's fine. Just let me know."

That night, I visited Daddy at the Homeplace, and I said, "Mama used to talk to me about Jesus, and now I know who He is, and I got saved, and the pastor of the church where I go wants me to be on his TV program."

Daddy was quiet for a minute, then he said, "You just can't stay out of it, can you?"

I said, "What do you mean?"

"Well," he said, "first thing you wanted to do after you got out of the service was grow a ponytail. Then you joined that motorcycle gang and rode around with that bunch of idiots, living in that clubhouse and getting into all kinds of trouble. Then you told me you were ashamed of all that, and you ain't going to do that no more. Now you want to go on TV and tell everybody you did it; you want to tell everybody what a sorry mess you are.

"You shouldn't do it. In the first place, the Bandidos will find out you're here. They'll come and get even with you for leaving them in jail. In the second place, nobody will give you a job after they hear that story broadcast all over the area on TV. In the third place, the police will hound you and harass you just like they do the others. So, you better lay low and keep your mouth shut."

"Boy," I said, "that is wisdom if I ever heard it."

I told Morris that Daddy counseled me against it, and that I respected his judgment. "I don't think I'll do it," I said.

"All right," he said, "that's fine."

Morris didn't mention it again, but my spiritual life went nowhere. I mean, it went in reverse.

CHAPTER NINE

"Man, I was wrong about you."

Now hath God set the members every one of them in the body, as it hath pleased him.
                                                1 Corinthians 12:18

1971: Lubbock

Boxi's 441 Victor scooter backfired, burned his pants, and knocked a hole in his plastic leg. While he was in El Paso for repairs, I tended the liquor store for him, sitting behind the counter on the stool, chain-smoking, watching TV, taking in the money, and wondering why everything was a drag. Even the liquor business was slow. Trying to be friends with the old lifestyle was bringing me down.

Kathleen was busy.

Pastor Morris Sheats was leaving me alone, but he and God were watching. One Wednesday evening after church, he said, "Johnny, my wife Janet and our daughter are going to be in Dallas this weekend. Why don't you come to our house? We'll "bach" it for a few days with Little Morris."

"Okay," I said. "Sounds good."

Friday evening at his home, we tried to talk, but his phone kept ringing—all kinds of people calling him for help. At one o'clock in the morning, he took the phone off the hook, and we went to bed.

Delivered

On Saturday, as soon as he put the receiver back on the hook, the phone rang. When we left to take Little Morris to the park, it was ringing again.

In the park some typical West Texas high-school kids in Levis and tank tops were sitting on the grass not far from us, when a police car pulled up. An officer got out and walked over to them. After talking to them for a few minutes, he led one of the girls to the police car. She got in the back seat, and they drove away.

Morris said, "Let's go see about that."

We walked over to the group and asked them what had happened. It was nothing new. The girl had been out all night. Her parents had called the police, and they had picked her up. I was glad the Bandidos hadn't got to her first. The kids told us where she lived—a nice middle-class neighborhood on the west side of town. When we got there, the girl's distraught and teary mother was coming out the front door.

Morris introduced himself, told her we had seen the officer arrest her daughter, and asked if there was anything we could do to help. "Can I pray for you right now?" he asked.

"No," she said. "I've got to hurry. My daughter . . ." Her voice trailed off as she choked back the tears and hurried to her car.

"Let's pray," Morris said. We bowed our heads as we stood on the sidewalk in front of the house and asked God to bless the whole family.

I was amazed by this man. Morris knew nothing about them except that they had a need, and he had come to meet it if he could. He was living what he preached from the pulpit.

When we finally returned to his house in the late afternoon, the phone was ringing. He answered, counselled the person on the other end, then said to me as he

Man, I was wrong about you.

was hanging up, "By the way, Johnny, you're my guest on the show this afternoon."

"What show?"

"My TV show, *'Rap.'* You're going to give your testimony. And since it starts at 6 o'clock, we better get on down there."

We made it through the interview. I gave my testimony again and tried to say what I was feeling, but since I had been saved such a short time, it was pretty rough. Soon it was over, and Morris was satisfied.

The people at Trinity Church raved about the show. Alton Summerall, a member of Trinity and also president of the Full Gospel Business Men's Lubbock chapter, invited me to speak at their meeting.

I said, "What's going on?"

And the devil answered. He said, "I used to think you were too sorry to get saved. Then I thought you were too sorry to stay saved. But, man, I was wrong about you. You really are a pretty good old boy. As a matter of fact, you are about the most spiritual guy around here." He was telling me I was God's gift to the church, specifically Trinity Church, and I was listening and agreeing with every word.

But Morris, who does not have a shooting-star syndrome, is not impressed with how bad a guy has been; he's only impressed with how good Jesus is. He was not about to raise me up and make a religious freak out of a sorry dog God was working with. Morris kept me under his wing and kept an eye on my ego.

"Johnny," he said, "I need someone to help me with an assignment. I think you're the man."

He probably wants me to take over one of his services, I thought, and I said, "Sure, Morris. Anything."

"I want you to paint the church," he said, "with a brush."

Delivered

When I got home on Monday, Boxi said, "Hey, man, I saw you on *'Rap.'* "

"Oh, yeah," I answered, "I'm a Christian now."

My initial conversion had made little impression on Boxi. The only difference he saw was that I had stopped drinking. I still jumped at every creak and rattle. He had no way of knowing that, when I stayed out all night, I was at the Living Room reading my Bible. At home I still tried to be good old Johnny.

Boxi didn't want to talk about my conversion, but after the program, it became easy for me to talk with the others who came to our house. I'd pull out a cigarette, deal out the poker hand and brag about what Jesus had done in my life.

Soon the wives began pressuring the men: "If Johnny can stop drinking, why can't you? Our kids are suffering." The guys soon became offended, and I had to back off.

One day, Morris said to me, "You know Dick Krycheck, don't you, Johnny? He was one of the counselors who prayed with you when you got saved. He's living alone in a trailer across from the airport, and if you want to get involved in his helps ministry, you can move in with him."

"What's a helps ministry?"

"Painting houses, cleaning yards, helping the widows and whoever else can't afford to hire professionals, doing whatever they need, and they pay what they can afford. How about it? Shall I call him?"

"Yeah, call him."

I moved in with Dick Krycheck, and we began meeting with some others for prayer every morning at six o'clock. Within two weeks, we had prayed ourselves into a burden for a halfway house to help other guys like I had been helped by moving in with Dick. We needed a

Man, I was wrong about you.

house, where we could minister to guys who got saved, and then had no place to go but back to their same problems.

We found it on a corner lot, a six-room, white-frame house, which we christened the Christian Bachelors Quarters, the CBQ. When I went back to Boxi's lake house to collect my few possessions—my TV and my painting—I felt like an alien. After living with Christians for only two weeks, I didn't feel at home there at all anymore.

Morris called me at the CBQ the next morning and said, "I've got a guy here at the church. His sister brought him over here two days ago. All he does is sit and stare at the floor. His name is Mike, and he needs help. Can he move in there for awhile?"

I said, "You bet."

We got Mike, brought him home, and introduced him to Jesus.

Morris called again. "Johnny, there's a sixteen-year-old boy at the Living Room named Tony. He's been strung out on heroin for two years, came off it cold turkey in the Yuma jail. His folks sent him here to an uncle who's in AA, and they want to try that program on him. Can you come over and talk to him?"

Dick and I went right over. "How're you doing, kid?"

No answer.

"Here, let's take a look at your arms. Roll up your sleeves."

He held his arms out, and we pushed up his sleeves.

"My God, look at that. Looks like somebody took a blowtorch to them."

It's one thing to be rapping with somebody who is talking back, even arguing, but this kid just didn't seem to be at home. Anyway, I felt in my heart that if I would pray for the boy, God would heal him.

Delivered

Okay, God, if crying is praying, I'll pray. What else can I do?

On the floor watching us, with eyes wide and brimming with tears, was a girl who had been an old lady for one of the Hell's Angels. God had already touched her life, and she knew He could help Tony. She inched over and laid her hand on his knee, as Dick and I knelt around him and prayed. Nothing happened. After awhile, the boy's uncle came in and took him home, and we went back to the CBQ.

The next morning Dick could see I was down.

"Come on, Johnny," he said, "let's go out to that uncle's farm and see that kid again. Maybe we can get through to him today."

At the farm, we asked the boy's uncle, "Where's Tony?"

"Plowing."

"Plowing? He must have got up this morning feeling pretty good. Where's he plowing?"

"Down that dirt road about a half mile. He's out there running middles."

The boy was half way down one of the rows when he saw us. He stopped the tractor, jumped off, and ran towards us, waving his bare arms.

"Dick," I said, "look at that, a heroin addict wearing a short-sleeved shirt!"

Tony was laughing and crying as he ran to us, threw his arms around both of us at the same time. Then he held his arms out and said, "Look! Look!"

Both arms were clean and dry, like they had been healed for years. Right then and there in the middle of the cotton field, we got down on our knees and thanked God, and praised Him, while Tony turned over his life to Jesus the Healer.

A few weeks later, a woman called and said, "Can

Man, I was wrong about you.

you help my grandson Steve? His father is in prison, his mother is in an asylum, and he's here. I don't know what to do with him."

We drove to the woman's house and found Steve, a listless, 80-pound skeleton virtually bloodless from five years' addiction to speed, lying limp on the worn sofa. He had dirty teeth, long, thick, dirty hair, and dirty blue circles around his sunken eyes.

"Steve," I said, "I'm Johnny Moffitt, and this here is Dick Krycheck."

Fear hit him like a blow.

"Steve, we ain't going to hurt you, boy. We want you to come live with us, to see if God can straighten out your life. You don't have to be like this—barefoot and dirty. You don't have to take drugs. We love you and want to help you. Will you come with us?"

Steve looked fearfully at his grandmother, who nodded her head.

We stuffed his ragged tee shirts and Levis into a brown paper sack, while he dragged himself up off the couch. Then, we drove with him to the CBQ. He seemed to be paranoid, afraid of us, even as we kept telling him about Jesus, and that we would take care of him.

Finally, he asked me, "Who did you say you are?"

"Johnny Moffitt."

"Moffitt?"

"Yeah, why? Anything the matter with Moffitt?"

"Whew!" he said, settling back in relief. "I thought you said Mafia."

Steve gave his heart to the Lord, gained weight, gained color, and wore out a rocking chair, rocking and reading His Bible.

I, too, had become a compulsive Bible reader. I helped at the Living Room, counselled at the CBQ, brought hitchhikers home, then dug into the Word of God for

Delivered

the answers to their questions, and found answers to many of my own. I kept up my marks at Draughan's to keep my GI benefits coming, so I could use the money in the Lord's work.

I had racked up an amazingly eventful two months: On the last Sunday of March, I got saved. I spent the last weekend of April with Morris. Then, during the last week in May, the dean of Draughan's called me into his office.

Uh oh, I thought, *I wonder what I've done. The last time a dean called me in, he asked me to leave school.*

The dean said, "Johnny, you're a different person these days. Something has happened in your life."

He waited for my response, but since I couldn't think of anything to say, I didn't say anything.

He continued. "I think you have leadership ability, and I want you to consider running for president of the student body in the June election in two weeks."

I gaped at him. "Me!? Are you sure?"

"Yes," he said, "I'm sure. Your friend Kathleen will be running for secretary. Think about it. Let me know what you decide to do."

I did think about it, and Kathleen and I were both elected.

Boxi's birthday was also in June, and I was invited to the party at the lake house. I wanted to go just to witness to my old friends about the Lord, but since I didn't want to go alone, I convinced Kathleen that, if she would go with me, we'd stay just a short time and then leave.

A pounding rock-and-roll beat met us at the top of the hill, and the stench of beer and stale marijuana assailed us as we drove down to the house. When I opened the door, I was shocked. The inside of the house had always been light enough for me before. But, this time we both had to fumble our way in toward the blaring loud-

Man, I was wrong about you.

speakers before our eyes adjusted somewhat to the gloom.

The party was loud and wild. People were yelling and laughing, standing near the wet bar, and lying around on pillows on the floor. I tried to introduce Kathleen to my old friends, but when one of the girls offered her a drink, she backed up and huddled in a corner. In about three minutes, she was out the door. I hung around for about ten more minutes, then I went out, and got into the car next to her. We sat there in heavy silence.

Then I said, "You ain't even friendly."

"I couldn't stand being in that place."

"What's the matter with that place?"

"The first thing I saw in there was that Buddha—like a shrine. That's evil."

"They ain't worshipping that plastic Buddha. It's just a statue. Listen, Kathleen, those are my friends; I've known them since third grade. What am I supposed to do, tell 'em that now, since I'm a Christian, I hate 'em? What kind of testimony is that?"

"Johnny, I don't think it's funny when somebody uses his wooden leg for an ashtray."

"That guy's been through plenty, and you ain't never going to catch him feeling sorry for himself."

"Okay, Johnny, but that's no place for you. You've got to separate yourself altogether from your old life. You just aren't spiritually strong enough."

"You are not trying to see my point of view," I said.

"And you're not trying to see mine. You've got to live a separated life, or you're going to go right back to what you were."

"Well, maybe that ain't such a bad idea."

"Oh, Johnny, don't talk stupid. Let's go home."

"Kathleen," I said, "Jesus doesn't hate those people.

Delivered

He loves them. How are they going to know that unless I tell them?"

"You can tell them, Johnny, but not now. It is just not the right time. They wouldn't listen."

We sat there in silence. Finally, I said, "Okay! Maybe you're right. I ain't putting 'em down, and I ain't turning my back on 'em, but I guess it ain't the right time. Let's go."

CHAPTER TEN

"What do you mean, accident?"

*The righteous perisheth, and no man layeth it to heart
... none considering that the righteous is taken away
from the evil to come. He shall enter into peace.*
Isaiah 57:1,2a

1971-1972: Lubbock

When Oscar Corley died in July, Kathleen and I drove Daddy to the funeral in Tahoka. Daddy and I had no precedent for beating around the bush, so while we were there, I said, "Daddy, if something happened to you, would you go to heaven or to hell?"

He answered immediately, "I would go to be with your mother."

"Are you sure, Daddy? Have you accepted Jesus as your personal Savior?"

"Johnny," he said, motioning towards the cafe, "come on in here. I want to tell you a story."

Kathleen, Daddy and I went in, sat down at a table, and ordered coffee. Daddy then told us in detail a story about an old friend who was dying, who insisted on having his underwear changed quickly, because the Lord was coming for him. As soon as the last button on his clean union-suit was fastened, the old man died.

When he was finished, I said, "Daddy, what in the world had that got to do with what I asked you?"

Daddy sat there in the cafe, fingering his coffee mug,

Delivered

and flicking his cigarette ashes onto the floor. Then he said, "I don't know. Got time to go fishing?"

"No, Daddy, we don't. We got to be getting on home."

On the way back, I tried in vain to figure out some way to connect Daddy's answer with my question. Kathleen suggested that maybe it was Daddy's way of saying he believed in Jesus, but didn't want to discuss doctrine with me.

Back at the CBQ, Dick announced that, as soon as we did one more job, he was leaving to get married.

"What's the job?"

"We're going to paint that old farmhouse on Lamar Forrest's daddy's ranch with this bright red paint."

"Nah, we ain't," I said. "Nobody but a drunk Mescan would paint a house that color. That's terrible!"

"Well, what do you care?" Dick said. "It isn't your house. This is the paint Lamar gave us, and this is what we're going to use."

"Well, I still think it's terrible, but let's get it done."

We painted the house, Dick moved out, and Nathan Knight moved in. Nathan, his fiancee Marsha, and a couple named Lowell and Carolyn Bryan were musicians. With their singing and my preaching, we formed a ministry team which we called "A Voice in the Wilderness." Wherever we were welcome, we went—to churches, retreats, street corners, jails and high-school assemblies. In our first meeting in a jail, seven prisoners and a guard gave their hearts to Jesus.

When we talked about drugs in the high schools, the kids, with tears streaming down their cheeks, came down front and piled their stuff on the stage: pot, cocaine, hash, uppers, downers, LSD, heroin, rigs—fortunes in illegal merchandise which we turned over to the authorities who were amazed.

We had a panel discussion on "Rap": the student-

What do you mean, accident?

presidents of Lubbock Christian College, Texas Tech University, Lubbock High School, and Draughan's Business College (me) talked to students about the problems they were facing, problems their parents didn't have to face at their age—promiscuity and drug abuse—sin with a capital S. Principals of high schools called Morris for help. Morris called us, and we went. The authorities wanted to know what would work, and we came and told them what had worked for us—Jesus.

We came home to the CBQ after a meeting one night to discover someone had broken into the house, thrown the silverware and linens into the middle of the living room, shattered one painting, and stretched the canvas of the blue ships by beating it over the back of a chair. Nothing seemed to be stolen, but the whole house was vandalized. We were making somebody mad.

Then one night in February, the phone rang. It was my oldest brother calling from Dallas. "Johnny Wade," he said, "Joel has been in an accident."

"What do you mean, accident? What happened? How is he?"

I heard him sigh on the other end of the line. "He didn't make it."

"That ain't true!"

"Yeah, it is, Johnny. Joel's dead. I thought you'd want to get on down here."

"Yeah," I said, and hung up.

The guys were watching me as I hung up the phone. "You okay, Johnny?"

"Yeah, I'm okay. Joel, my brother's kid—he's dead. Twelve years old and he's dead. I've got to go to Dallas."

"You got any money, Johnny?"

"No."

"Here, you can have this. It's all I got."

"You can use my car, Johnny."

Delivered

"Want me to go with you?"

I looked around at the guys, and I thought, *You guys must have come straight out of God's heart.*

In Dallas, when I went with Stanley to the funeral home, he told what had happened.

Joel had been visiting his Christian friend Scott across the street. He was coming home on his bike, cutting through his own front yard, when a man driving a pickup truck lost control.

The driver's mentally handicapped daughter had dropped something on the floor of the truck, and he was reaching down to help her pull it back up onto the seat. He was in a hurry. He was also very drunk.

The truck angled across the road through the shallow ditch and into the yard. It smashed into Joel on his bicycle, then went on past him, shearing off a telephone pole about a foot above the ground, leaving the top half dangling from the wires. Twenty feet beyond the pole the truck came to a stop.

Scott, who had watched the whole thing from his own front yard, flew across the street, grabbed Joel up into his arms and started praying, but it was too late. Joel said, "Uhn," one time, and died in his arms.

Two weeks before, over Joel's protest, Scott had badgered him into going with him and his family to the Billy Graham Crusade.

Joel had said, "Scott, I don't want to go to that religious meeting."

But Scott cajoled. "Come on, Joel. You might like it."
"I don't want to go."
"You like football, don't you?"
"What kind of a question is that? You know I do."
"Well, guess where the crusade is going to be held?"
"Where?"
"At the brand new, never-before-used Texas Stadium, where the Dallas Cowboys will be playing football."

What do you mean, accident?

"No kidding?"
"No kidding! Now, will you go?"
"Okay, I'll go, but just to see the stadium. Yippee!"

Two days before the funeral, Sue opened a letter in the mail addressed to Joel. She read it, then handed it to me. "Here, Johnny. You'll be interested in this."

I was. The letter said in part:

Dear Joel,

It was a privilege and a joy to talk to you about your decision to dedicate your life to Jesus Christ. I am sure you will look back on September 26, 1971, many times as a most meaningful day in your life. I hope you have started to read the Gospel of John that I gave you, and spend some time each day in prayer. The things that concern us, concern Him.
Please feel free to contact me if I can be of any help.

Your friend in Christ,

It was signed by one of the crusade counselors.

Three-year-old Michelle was asking, "Daddy, where's Bubba?"

"I don't know, Sugar," Stanley said. "I guess he's with Jesus."

I know he's with Jesus! I thought, but I was too choked up to say it out loud. *Yes, he's with Jesus!*

Joel's junior-high school retired his football number, then folded his jersey, and placed it with a plaque in the trophy case. The members of the team were honorary pallbearers.

On the way to the cemetery in the family limousine, Michelle stared out the window, her eyes too big and too sad for such a little girl. She was crying silently.

Delivered

"Daddy?"

"What is it, Baby?"

"Daddy, where's Bubba?"

Nobody said anything. Sue began to whimper.

"Daddy, is Bubba dead?"

Sue hunched over. Her shoulders began to shake as the sobs she had tried to suppress rolled out of her tired and aching heart.

Michelle began to sob.

Stanley groaned as tears poured down his cheeks. Did he really believe that Joel was with Jesus? I was the Christian. I was supposed to be strong, to support them, but I was too burdened with my own grief. *Why, Jesus? Why?* And I saw how ruthless the enemy is, and I determined to fight him to my last breath.

In August, back in Lubbock, Kathleen announced that she was moving to Dallas. Not until then had I realized how much I had come to depend on her. And then, she was gone.

In November, at the end of the school quarter, I decided not to run for reelection. A week before Christmas, I dropped out of school altogether. Just like the old Johnny, I quit.

Even though "A Voice in the Wilderness" still ministered somewhere every week, I was preaching all the time, saturating myself with the Word of God, and keeping busy at the church and at the CBQ. But something was missing. I had more real friends than I could keep up with, more than I ever thought possible, but for some reason it wasn't enough.

"We're going to pray you up a wife," said Marsha and Nathan.

"Yeah, sure!" I said. "I'm sure that's all I need—a wife!"

"That's exactly what you need!" they said. "A wife!"

CHAPTER ELEVEN

"I think we'll just break the date."

It is not good that the man should be alone.
                                               Genesis 2:18

1972: Lubbock

During the 1972 New Year's Day party at Trinity Church, I watched a pretty girl go through the buffet line, scan the four-hundred faces around her, then beeline for a chair near mine. She pulled it over next to me, sat down, and said, "Hi! I'm Betty Harris."

Nice friendly girl, I thought. *Pretty, too—nice clothes, good figure, kinda short, old-fashioned looking with her hair pulled back like that, and her prim little mouth makes her eyes look big. Pretty girl.*

I was getting ready to leave and, since she didn't say anything else, neither did I.

After that I saw her occasionally at the church with Terry, a little towheaded boy about three years old, and I assumed that if she was somebody's mother, she was probably somebody's wife.

At noon one day, while Betty was waiting in the Living Room for a Bible study to begin, I walked over to her, sat down, and said, "There's an outpouring of the Holy Spirit at the Southcrest Baptist Church. Would you and your husband like to go with me tonight?"

She said, "I don't have a husband."

"Well, okay," I said, "then will you go with me?"

Delivered

"Yes, I will, and I knew you were going to ask me that before you came into the room."

"How did you know? I didn't even know."

"I don't know how I knew. I just knew."

When I got home from work the next day, Betty brought over a ham. From then on, wherever Betty was, that was where I wanted to be. We saw each other every day through the rest of February and the first three weeks of March.

One Saturday, when I was washing my car in the driveway and Betty was inside cooking for us (I thought), Steve caught her in my room.

"Betty, what are you doing in there?"

"Cleaning his room."

"You don't know what you're doing! Johnny is going to be furious!"

"He's not going to be mad at me."

"He won't be able to find anything. You've never seen him mad. You don't know what you're doing."

"You already said that. Come here, Steve. Look out this window. See him out there in those ratty cutoffs and those old stinky sandals standing in the back of that beat-up convertible hosing down the insides of that old car? If I can feel this good about him when he looks that bad, it must be love. And he is not going to be mad at me for cleaning his room."

On Friday at noon, Betty said, "Johnny, I keep having these thoughts about 'when we get married,' and I keep rebuking them, but they don't go away. Maybe we should get married."

I said, "Okay, I've been having the same thoughts. You pray about it, and I'll pray about it, and we'll see what we come up with. Meanwhile, tonight we start a two-day revival in Abernathy."

The next morning I went to the workplace for her

I think we'll just break the date.

answer, and to take her out for lunch.

"Well, Betty," I said, "what have you decided?"

"I don't know," she said. "I don't know that much about how to hear the Lord's voice. I've only been baptized in the Holy Spirit for three months. What do you think?"

I said, "The Lord told me we're supposed to get married."

She said, "Well, if the Lord told you, I guess we are, then."

I said, "We're supposed to get married on Monday."

Betty said, "Well, okay. I guess we are, then."

"Tell your boss you need the rest of today off to get a ring," I said to Betty, "and then let's tell your folks."

"Mom probably already knows. They're going to California on Monday."

I didn't stop to wonder how I could take care of a wife, who had a son and a dog, when I had no money, no job, and no place to live. We were too busy getting the ring, lining up the preacher, and preparing for the second and last night of the revival in Abernathy to worry about details.

"Betty, are you ready? My, you sure do look pretty."

"It's the dress."

"Is that a new dress? Where'd you get that?"

"Mom bought it for me this afternoon. It's my wedding dress. She said I needed a new dress to get married in on Monday, and I didn't know what else to wear tonight."

On the way back from Abernathy that night, Betty said, "Johnny, look at this. A man at the meeting came up to me and said, 'The Lord told me to give this to you,' and he handed me this twenty-dollar bill."

I said, "Look at this. A guy who's been owing me a hundred dollars for months picked tonight to pay it

Delivered

back."

The next day, Sunday, within an hour after the close of the worship service, one of the elders of the church asked me if I would like a job doing some construction for him.

"Yeah," I said, "I'd like to hammer some nails."

As I was turning around to tell Betty, Lamar Forrest offered me the use of the little farmhouse on the Forrest Ranch rent free plus a little cash to keep an eye on the automatic sprinkler systems in the pastures behind it.

"The two-bedroom house we painted for you, Lamar?"

"That's the one."

"The red house?"

"Yeah, you know the house. Are you interested?"

"Yeah, we're interested. We'll take it. Thanks."

The red house was empty except for a lopsided butane cook stove, a vintage refrigerator, and the resident mice. On Sunday afternoon, Betty stayed there wielding bucket and broom, while I collected furniture—the chest I had when I was a child, a black walnut table I had made in high school, a blue sectional sofa, a wobbly, green formica and chrome dinette set, an ancient green reclining chair with its own argot of squeaks and squawks, two matching table lamps, a double bed for us, a single bed for Terry, my misshapen boat painting, and my TV set.

Betty said, "Johnny, can you straighten up this stove? If I ever bake you a cake, it'll look like a hillside."

"I'll fix it."

"Johnny, what's that terrible noise?"

"It's nothing, just the cows scratching their necks on the corner of the house."

"This kitchen cabinet is so small, I can only get three plates and three glasses in it."

I think we'll just break the date.

"Well, there's only going to be three of us."

"Johnny, this house doesn't feel stable. If there was a big sand storm, it would fall right off the cinder blocks."

"If there is a storm, we'll just open the windows, and let the sand blow right on through. Are you through cleaning up?"

"I'm through."

"Do you like it?"

"I love it."

The wedding was set for Monday at noon so Betty's brother could attend during his lunch break. Betty's father Joe hauled his TV-repair paraphernalia out of the den so Betty and her mother could clean and decorate with a few flowers. But on Monday morning, Hazel panicked. There was no wedding cake. She raced to the bakery to order one.

"When will you want this, Mrs. Harris?"

"In an hour."

"An hour? We can't make a wedding cake in an hour!"

"I know you've got something around here to make a wedding cake," she said, "a sheet cake or something. I've got to have it in an hour, and I know you can do it. I'll be back."

She was back in an hour, and she brought the cake home.

I said, "Hazel, it's probably got 'Happy Bar Mitzvah, Bernie' written across the top."

"It does not!" she said. "It's beautiful. Now, just get on out of my way; I've got things to do."

Pastor Graham, Nathan and Marsha, Betty's sister Donna and her husband, and some others were in the den talking quietly at noon, when Betty's brother came in from work, cleaned the grease off his hands, changed his clothes, and joined us.

Just before the ceremony, Betty said, "Somebody,

Delivered

please tape this. If I forget to do something I promise to do, Johnny will want to play it back to me."

Donna cried through the whole ceremony.

During the wedding feast of ham sandwiches and Fritos, coffee and cake, Joe said, "You two can have your honeymoon here if you want to. We're already packed to go to California this afternoon, and we're taking Terry with us."

"Donna, stop crying," Betty said. "After all, I'm only going to be just down the road."

"I'm not crying about you," Donna said between sniffles. "I don't want Mama and Daddy to leave me behind. I want to go to California, too."

CHAPTER TWELVE

"I like having you home."

For the eyes of the Lord run to and fro throughout the whole earth, to show himself strong in the behalf of them whose heart is perfect towards him.
                                         2 Chronicles 16:9

1972: Lubbock

The Forrest Ranch comprised two 7,000-acre ranges, one in Colorado and the other in Texas. The red farmhouse stood in the 320-acre half-section in Texas known as the breed farm.

It was a breed farm all right. We bred not only cows, but also horseflies. The day after Betty and I moved in, there was a hatch. The ceiling was black with them. I sprayed, while Betty vacuumed.

My responsibility to Lamar, in exchange for the use of the red house, was to operate two huge sprinkler systems, each of which watered a half-mile circle of flat pasture on the breed farm. The sprinklers looked like enormous, elongated, wingless, transparent, many-segmented insects. Each consisted of twelve-foot connected lengths of galvanized water pipe topped with rows of water jets, moving on pairs of four-foot-long pipe legs on wheels. All of this rotated from a central stationary pump. Each system had its own well. My job was to turn the power on and off, to regulate the speed, and to make sure they were both operating properly. That still left

Delivered

plenty of time for me to work a full day with the construction company.

Meanwhile, Hazel took care of Terry while Betty worked at Skaggs packaging meat. After work, Betty would pick me up, then we would get Terry and go home, where Betty would fix dinner while I read my Bible. This went on for weeks.

One night, Betty said, "Johnny, when are you going to fix the front-door latch?"

"I'll fix it."

"You've been saying that for six weeks, and all you do is sit there smoking those stinky cigarettes and reading your Bible. How many times have you read it through?"

"This is the seventh time. I've read The Living Bible twice, and this is the fifth time for the King James. If I'm going to be a preacher, I've got to know what it says."

"But, Johnny," Betty said, "since we've been married not one single person or church has called you to preach and you used to preach two or three times a week at least."

"Yeah," I said. "I've noticed. Kinda depressing, ain't it?"

"I don't think so because I like having you home even if you don't ever do anything but read."

"Why don't you read?"

"I can't read and fix your dinner at the same time so I got these tapes from the church and they're on faith because I want to have more faith."

"Okay," I said, "you listen to the tapes, and I'll read."

One morning, Betty said, "Johnny, I can read the Post Toasties box across the room with my glasses off."

"So?"

"I have faith to be healed."

"What are you talking about, girl?"

"God's going to heal my eyes so I don't need my

I like having you home.

glasses or contacts anymore and I'm going to burn them."

"Are you sure you don't need them anymore?"

"I have faith. That's what those tapes are about."

"Betty, have you heard from God about this? Contacts are expensive."

"It's God's Word and He can't lie and it says that if I ask anything believing I can have it. I can see without my glasses. I don't need them anymore. God has healed me."

"Well, if you're sure it's God."

Betty burned her glasses and contact lenses in an act of faith. She took them out to the 55-gallon trash-burner and burned them. Then, she couldn't see to drive, and she kept bumping into the doorjambs, and burning herself at the stove.

During the whole next month, when I had to drive her to work, she kept saying, "Don't worry about me. I've got faith to be healed."

"Yeah, but you're going to kill yourself first."

"My not being able to see is just a lying symptom of the devil."

"Well, my having to drive you to work is no lying symptom, and I'm getting tired of it. Let's get you some glasses."

She got the glasses and kept listening to the tapes.

Then one day, I came in the house and found blood all over the floor and a note from Betty: "Don't worry about the blood. We've gone to mother's."

What did she mean, she'd gone to mother's? Had she left me? I called the Harris house.

Betty answered. "I'm crippled, Johnny. I can't walk."

"You what? What do you mean, you can't walk?"

"I was cutting the grass out behind the house thinking about black widow spiders biting Terry or maybe me when the lawn mower hit a piece of bailing wire and

Delivered

it wrapped itself around the blade and whipped me across the heel and that's where the blood came from. We're over at mother's."

"I know where you are. How did you get there?"

"Well, when I cut my ankle I grabbed my leg and said, 'Oh, God, when you cut one of those big veins you die.' So, I called mother and she came and took me to the hospital and I sat in the emergency room an hour and almost bled to death before anybody told the doctor I was there. And, Johnny, I looked terrible. I had on my brother's big baggy tee shirt with grass all over my legs..."

"Are you all right?"

"Well, I'm not supposed to walk. You'll have to carry me."

"I'm coming over there. I'll be there in a few minutes."

I carried Betty for a week, then we rented a wheelchair.

In the car one day on the way to church, we listened to one of the tapes. "Believe God," the man said. "Decide when you want God to do it; set a time for it."

Betty said, "Johnny, without faith it is impossible to please God and I don't have any faith and I can't please God and I'm a wretched thing and I'm just so blown away I don't know what to do."

I didn't know what to tell her.

After church that night, as I was wheeling her out to the parking lot, a man stopped us and said to her, "Betty, I saw you in the spirit. You were getting up out of this chair. If you will just act on this and get up, God will heal you. God has healed you. Now, act on your faith." And he began to pray in tongues.

Betty forced herself up from the wheelchair. She stiffened her legs, and walked to the car.

There was a murmur of joy from the crowd.

I like having you home.

"Oh, praise God!"
"She can walk!"
"She's been healed!"
I didn't know what to think.

Betty cried in agony all the way home. She was not healed. She said, "The man who said that to me was the same one who gave me the twenty-dollar bill in Abernathy that night and I didn't want to embarrass him. Oh, Johnny, it hurts so bad. Why don't I have the faith for God to heal me, Johnny? What's wrong with my faith? Where's my faith? What's wrong with me?"

"Betty, we are going to talk to Morris about this. I've never heard him preach what you are hearing on those tapes. We are going to talk to him tomorrow."

The next day in Morris' office, Betty said, "Morris, what's wrong with my faith? That man yesterday heard from God. God told him to tell me that, so it had to be true. It was prophecy. He was speaking in tongues. And prophecy and tongues, they're all from God, so how could it not happen? Why was I not healed?"

Morris said, "Betty, listen to me. I'm going to tell you something that is very important for you to understand. Just this: Betty, God loves you. That's what He wants you to know."

Betty had hoped that Morris would lay hands on her, rebuke something, tell her that she didn't have enough faith but that he did, and heal her. She thought he had not understood what she was trying to say.

Later, I went to talk to an elder about it, who said, "Morris is right. God's love—that's the most important thing, not whether we get healed on cue. Faith needs to grow, so that all areas of our lives keep in step. We are alive only by the grace of God. We are His servants, He's not ours. God's not impressed by Betty's burning her glasses. When she's healed, she won't be able to see with them on. There's nothing wrong with the tapes, but they

Delivered

are spiritual meat, and you're both still on the bottle."

We traded Betty's wheelchair for crutches. She used them for a month, then returned because she didn't need them anymore. Because God healed her.

We discovered that for us formulas didn't work. We could rebuke the devil, claim Scripture, and confess positive till we turned green. But, when we were healed, it was not because we rebuked the devil, claimed Scripture, and confessed positive—or even quoted Scripture to remind God of what He said in His Word. When we were healed, it was because in His love and His grace He healed us.

Daddy had retired. Then, in November, he died. He had been watching TV with a friend, had got up, and was walking across the room, when his heart stopped. It was that easy. I remembered what he told me about going to be with Mama. I could only trust that it was so.

There was a constant war on our faith. We never seemed to have enough money. Betty, who had quit work when she hurt her ankle, was pregnant. Terry got kicked in the face by a horse and got his nose broken. I got thrown from a horse and sprained my diaphragm again like I had in Puerto Rico. I ground Betty's new contacts up in the garbage disposal at her parents' home. A stray dog had puppies under our porch, and our cat had kittens in our closet. On top of all that, during a very cold night in the fall, the water in one of the sprinklers froze up and broke the pipes, and the whole system curled up like a tumbleweed.

Late in November, Lamar said, "Johnny, the Lord told me to let you go. I'll write you any kind of recommendation you want because this is in no way a reflection on your work. But you need to be out by the first of January because we're going to tear down the red house."

CHAPTER THIRTEEN

"God, You don't understand!"

They that wait upon the Lord shall renew their strength; they shall mount up with wings as eagles; they shall run, and not be weary; they shall walk, and not faint.   Isaiah 40:31

1972: Lubbock

Three weeks before Christmas, I fingered the lone five-dollar bill in my pocket and stared down the dirt turn-road out at the breed farm where I had learned so much from Lamar, from Betty and from God. Betty and I had followed up a help-wanted ad for house parents for a boys' home in Abilene, but they were looking for a couple with no children, especially without one on the way.

One year earlier, I hadn't even known Betty and Terry were in the world. Now they were my world, and I had five bucks, and Christmas was coming fast. For Betty's present, I would fix the front door latch and stay up all night installing the paneling that had been leaning against the wall for six months. *Nah! That's no present—we're leaving!*

Terry would be getting up on Christmas morning, too. What could I do for Terry?

Betty had taken the news about leaving with more grace than I could muster. She had said, "Johnny, Lamar

Delivered

is a man of God. If he says God told him to let you go, then God has something else for us."

I walked the half mile down the turn-road to the lone elm tree, and grabbed hold of the "charismatic cop-out," Romans 8:28:

"Okay, God, here's what You said: All things work together for good to those who love God, and are the called according to His purposes."

All things work together for good! All things work together for good! So, all things work together for good? I've got a hungry family and no money, and all things work together for good?!

I was sitting under that tree, bawling like a baby, and yelling at God: "All things work together for good!" The more I said it, the more I didn't believe it. It just wasn't true. I finally screamed out, "God, it's not true! All things do NOT work together for good! You just don't understand! You don't see what's going on down here. I've got no money, a pregnant wife, and I've got to be out of my house by the end of the month. And You're trying to tell me that all things work together for good? It's a lie!"

After a dead silence, when all I could hear was my own sniveling, the voice of God roared through my spirit to my brain, but it might just as well have been through my ears to my brain, it was that loud.

"Fat Boy, that is a promise, not a pacifier."

His voice rocked me. I sat paralyzed, not daring to breath, then heard myself murmuring softly, "All things work together for good."

And God opened my eyes. I looked, and through my spirit to my brain, but it might just as well have been through my eyes to my brain, I saw the Texas Boys Ranch right in front of me. I saw a beautiful brick home for boys—pre-delinquent, non-achiever boys from the courts, who were headed for death or prison or maybe

God, You don't understand!

motorcycle gangs. It was right there behind the tree in front of my eyes, as though it had already been built.

I jumped to my feet and ran back to the house, shouting, "Betty! Betty! Betty!"

"My goodness, Johnny, what are you yelling about? What on earth is the matter?"

"Betty!" I was puffing hard. I could hardly talk. "Betty, God showed me we're going to build a boys ranch."

"Well, that's wonderful, Johnny, but how are we going to do that?"

"I don't know," I said. "I jumped and run before He had a chance to show me."

CHAPTER FOURTEEN

"Go see Alvin Shambeck."

Pass through the host . . . to go in to possess the land, which the Lord your God giveth you to possess it.
Joshua 1:11a,c

1973-1974: Lubbock

Just as clearly as God had called me Fat Boy, He said, "Go see Alvin Shambeck."

I rang Alvin's front-door bell. Surprised to see me standing there, he said, "Johnny, I've just been thinking about you."

"Alvin," I said, "God told me to build a boys ranch, and I don't know how to do it."

Alvin said, "I do. Come on in. Let's talk about it."

We sat in his office, and he said, "Johnny, if the Lord told you to do this, don't let anything or anyone stop you. Now, the first thing you need to do is let the people know."

The first one we let know was Morris.

On the 28th of December, twenty-seven men from Lubbock met informally in Lamar Forrest's home. As soon as I shared the vision with them, one of them stood up and said, "Let's do it."

We immediately elected a six-man board of directors, and called the first official meeting for January 15, 1973.

As we were getting ready to leave, Lamar called me

aside and said, "Johnny, have you found a place to move to yet?"

"Not yet, Lamar," I said, "but I've still got a couple of leads to check out."

"Well," Lamar said, "we've decided to leave the red house standing until later in the spring, so if you and Betty want to stay there until after the baby is born, you're welcome to."

Betty, who was very pregnant at the time, didn't want to move from our red honeymoon shack ever.

"Johnny," she said, "I love this place. Why do we have to leave at all? I love the cows rubbing their big, soft, wet noses on our bedroom window every morning. I love the designs Terry draws in the fresh sand on the living room floor every day."

"Because eventually they are going to tear it down and it won't be here."

At the January meeting, the board of directors agreed unanimously to put me on salary so that I could promote the project full-time.

Since we could not get a license to operate until we had the land, the building, a director, and enough money in the bank to operate for a full year, the first item on the agenda was to submit a proposed budget with an application for a Certificate of Authorization to Solicit Funds, to the Texas Department of Welfare.

Our first contribution, a check for $100, came from Leroy Deardorff, the man at Trinity Church in the $300 suit, who bear-hugged me the first time I went there with Kathleen. Two weeks after the initial board meeting, I opened an account with the Security National Bank of Lubbock with a $186 deposit.

We knew we couldn't do it alone, so we talked to everybody we knew. We walked down the streets and knocked on doors. We advertised in newspapers, then

Go see Alvin Shambeck.

published the *Circuit Rider*, a monthly newsletter, to let everybody who was interested keep up with what was going on. We told folks over secular radio that we knew God wanted the boys ranch, but we didn't have any idea where it would be built. As soon as the news was out, we began receiving applications on behalf of boys who needed help.

The board sent me to the Colorado Boys Ranch in La Junta, to Cal Farley's Boys Ranch in Amarillo, and to the National Association of Homes for Boys convention in Detroit, to meet people, to talk to people, to collect brochures, charters, bylaws, corporation procedures, and records of everything they were doing, so we could benefit from their experiences and avoid their mistakes.

On March 20th, I deposited Terry, Honey the dog and Sweetie the cat with Joe and Hazel, and took Betty to the hospital where Travis was born. Two weeks later, when we moved back to the red house, we discovered we had been robbed again. This time Betty was ready to move to town.

For five months, the TBR board members shopped for land, getting uptight chasing one wild-goose lead after another. Finally, at a board meeting one of the members stood up and said, "God is the One Who started this project. He knows that we need land to move on with it. Let's pray."

After a shuffling of chairs, eleven men went down on their knees.

A few days later, Edwin Forrest dropped in to see Alvin Shambeck. He had questions: "Do you think this project will go over with the public? Do you think the State will give you a license? Do you think a home will be built? Do you think there will ever be boys out there? If I give you the land, will there be enough money coming in to support it?"

Delivered

Yes, to all the above.

During this time, I only smoked cigarettes at home or in my car. I'd buy a pack, open it, take one out, light it, smoke half of it, get mad, throw it out the window, wad up the pack, throw it out the window, then stop and buy another pack. It was an expensive way to maintain a habit. Listerine and Certs were costing me a fortune, while I thought I was fooling people by hiding my yellowed fingers under my Bible.

Betty said, "We don't have enough money and I can't work and you're gone all the time and all you do when you're home is read and those stinky cigarettes are killing Terry and hurting my baby."

At the end of June, Bob Terrill from Graham, Texas, held a seminar for ministers at Trinity Church. With a pack of cigarettes as usual tucked into my right sock, I went on Saturday morning to hear him.

At the end of the morning session, Bob said, "We're not going to take time for special prayer this morning. We'll break for lunch, then come back this afternoon. Then, tonight we'll pray for people with special needs."

But God spoke to my heart. He said, "If you will go forward, and ask Bob to pray for you right now, I will deliver you from smoking."

I said, "Now, wait a minute, God. You can do this anytime—when I'm at home or in the car—but not now in front of all these preachers! I've held meetings in their churches! You don't want me to stand up and say, 'Look, I want to be delivered from smoking.' That would be like dropping a bomb right in the middle of this meeting. Why would You want me to do that? God, don't do it in front of all these people."

"Do you want to be free?"

So, I stood up and said, "Bob, God just told me that, if you would pray for me right now, He would deliver

Go see Alvin Shambeck.

me from smoking cigarettes." Accompanied by quiet gasps from around the room, I walked down to Bob, who laid his hand on my forehead.

I went down on the floor, and lay there, immobilized, thinking, *This is not the way things are supposed to be. This does not happen in the morning meeting before lunch.* But I never wanted the next cigarette.

Our application to the State for accreditation was refused. The board members had taken it for granted that I would be the director of the ranch, but because of my limited education, I did not qualify. Since the State required someone with at least a master's degree in Juvenile Justice, the board enrolled me in South Plains College in Levelland to take classes in Psychology and in Prejudice and Racism. I went back to school.

The board members said to me, "We know what the law says, but we also know we can get you a license. The question is, do you really want to direct this ranch?"

My enthusiasm for the ranch project never waned. I knew we would see the fruits of our labors, and I saw the money for the ranch rolling in, but I could not answer that question lightly, even though I knew the vision was from the Lord.

In April of 1974, we had a telethon, sharing our vision with the public, and showing them the drawings of the land, the hot-wire fence, the newly paved road, and the three flagpoles which had been donated by the American Legion. Janet Sheats, who was in charge, prayed down a two-inch rainfall so the people would not only be happy about their crops being watered, but also be inside their houses watching the celebrities and high-school bands demonstrating their support of the ranch over television. Within six hours, we received over $30,000 in cash donations, plus bricks, wood, sheetrock, nails, cement, wire—whatever we asked for.

Delivered

But at home we were miserable. There was never enough money.

Betty said, "Living with you is the pits."

She was overtired, overworked, disorganized and getting up two or three times every night with Travis, who was an infant and crying all the time. Terry was miserable and misbehaving. I was going to school mornings, working full-time for the ranch, and installing swimming pools part-time to make the payments on a 35-inch repossessed TV console that I sank in front of every time I walked in the front door. Betty and I were both exhausted. There was never enough of me left from my day to help her, and never enough of her left from her day to help me. We were not miserable with each other; we were just two miserable people.

We decided that part of our personal problem was that the red house was too small. In spite of our being worn-out and broke, we moved into a large, four-bedroom house with a beautiful blue carpet throughout, and a fenced yard. Even though we had lived in the red house for a year, we had never had enough energy or time to unpack, so we just loaded the boxes, and moved them again.

One night in the big house, we collapsed on the bed, both weeping from pure exhaustion, when there was a knock on the door. Betty dragged herself up to answer, and there stood Alvin Shambeck with a schoolboy grin on his face and two pies in his hands.

"I just stopped by to tell you that I love you," he said, as he handed the pies to Betty. Then he got into his Lincoln Continental and drove away. Betty and I started to laugh. We laughed and laughed because we knew that somehow God would work it all out.

One night at a board meeting, I stood up and said, "The simple fact is that, if we are going to run a boys

Go see Alvin Shambeck.

ranch, we have got to run it according to the law of the State. It's too complicated for me. I can keep the vision in front of the people, but when it comes down to teenagers with severe problems, I just don't have the training to handle it. We need to get serious about hiring somebody who is qualified."

We appointed a personnel committee, then advertised in the Child Care Journal, finally hiring a man about my age, whose master's degree was not in Juvenile Justice, but in Criminal Justice. He was capable and tough, but he didn't have the vision. His heart was in Corrections.

Therein lay the conflict. He was in charge, but I was the one who knew what was going on. I was the one who knew the people, who knew what questions had been asked, and what solutions had been found. I resented him because of his authority. He resented me because everybody came to me for answers. But he held the master's degree, and we got our license because of it.

CHAPTER FIFTEEN

"How would you like to move?"

See, I have this day set thee over the nations and over the kingdoms, to root out, and to pull down, and to destroy, and to throw down, to build, and to plant.
Jeremiah 1:10

1974-1975: Lubbock

The *llano estacado* of West Texas is so flat and treeless, so the saying goes, that a man has to drive a stake into the ground if he wants to tie his horse. And, in 1974, that was pretty much the way it was around Forrest Road.

During 1974 and 1975, Edwin Forrest, for whom the road was named, eventually donated the entire 320-acres piecemeal to the Texas Boys Ranch, Incorporated. The first parcel--15 acres deeded to the corporation in June-- was the breed farm, which bordered the center of the dirt road, and included the solitary elm, where I had had the vision.

Ground-breaking Day was August 14, 1974. We chartered a bus to bring some important people and the press out from town to the new fence and the paved road and the three flagpoles. After a few speeches, six men with gold-sprayed shovels turned some dirt, the people cheered and the press took pictures.

During the fall, we watched the construction of Cottage One, a hundred-thousand dollar, modern brick

Delivered

building designed to house ten pre-delinquent and neglected boys placed there by the jails or courts or churches or even by their own parents. The TBR also needed a staff house for the farm-ranch director (my new title) and his family (Betty and the boys). We found it at the South Plains Fair where First Manufactured Homes, Inc., offered us a deal on the carpeted, three-bedroom display model, which they could deliver at the end of February, one month before we were to move in.

On delivery day in February, I said to Betty, "How would you like to move?"

"That's a silly question," she said, "since we're already going to move to the ranch in a month."

"I mean, how would you like to move today?"

"Is the staff house hooked up and all ready for us?"

"No."

"Then I wouldn't. Why did you ask me that?"

"Because the people who own this house just sold it, and the new owners want to move in tomorrow."

"You mean move out of our nice house with the four bedrooms and the blue carpet and the fenced yard and the nice neighborhood and move our baby Travis and our little boy Terry and our cat and our dog and all their things and all our things for just one month and then move it all again to the staff house?"

"Yeah, it looks like it."

Betty sighed. "Let's pack."

We moved in with Hazel and Joe.

Ribbon-cutting Day for Cottage One, March 17, 1975, dawned in an orange-beige dust storm filtering up from the southwest with a cold wind driving sand, tumbleweeds and trash in a straight line across the barren fields. Visibility was little more than arm's length. That meant that Betty would be walking around all day with her eyes closed, a contact lens in each hand, fighting her

Would you like to move?

skirt to maintain a semblance of modesty. The rest of us, coated with a thin layer of sand, and feeling like we had been eating dirt, would grin and bear the cold and discomfort, while Morris pronounced the dedication. Then, with their right hands holding one pair of scissors, the director and the chairman of the board would cut the ribbon across the front door.

As soon as the ribbons fell, we rushed into the cottage out of the sand storm. We celebrated the official opening of the TBR with punch and cookies and the matchless talents of Little Jimmy Henley, the twelve-year-old world's champion banjo picker.

Jay and Pat Mathis, TBR's first set of house parents, had already moved in that morning. With the rest of us on TBR's original board of directors, they had weathered the legal red tape plus the unconcern and enthusiasm and vacillation and sacrifice of the public. They had sold their home in Lubbock along with most of their household possessions and their machine-tool business to help bring to birth the TBR and make it their home forever.

That same day, Betty and I and our two boys moved into the modern, six-room staff house, which stood a hundred feet north of where the little old red farm and honeymoon house had once leaned with the wind.

Later that night, when all was quiet, Betty said, "We've only known each other three years. You've changed."

"Why did you marry me, Betty?"

"You didn't give me any choice. On our second date, you were already bossing me like the honeymoon was over."

"That was Nathan and Marsha's fault. They were praying me up a wife."

Delivered

"You weren't very nice to me the first time I met you. You were rude to me."

"How was I rude?"

"Well, I thought all Spirit-filled Christians were perfect. But at the church party, when I didn't know anybody, and came over to introduce myself to you and some of the others, you got up and left me sitting there like a big, fat frog."

"I'm sorry, Betty. What did you do then?"

"I sat there, stared around for awhile, burped, then finally got up and went home."

"Have you forgiven me?"

"I married you, didn't I?"

"Yeah, and you know what's the best part of that?"

"What?"

"You broke a date to do it. What was his name?"

"Oh, Johnny, I don't remember."

"It was Bob . . ."

CHAPTER SIXTEEN

"You sure ain't allowed to cuss!"

Suffer the little children to come unto me, and forbid them not.   Mark 10:14

1975: Lubbock

God had given me the vision for the ranch only two years and four months earlier. Both cottage and property were debt free. It was a miracle.

Miracle or not, by June 20th I was ready to hang it up. Earlier in the month, I hired two welders to help me build some cow pens at the far end of the property. Because of continual interruptions the work was behind schedule when the director came down to see me.

"When are you going to be finished with this?" he asked.

"We'll be through in about a month," I replied.

"I want you to be through by the end of this week."

"Man, there ain't no way we can be done that fast. We'll hurry it up, but we can't be finished by then."

He said, "All right," then turned and left.

The following Tuesday afternoon, I parked the ranch pickup in the packed-dirt parking lot in front of Cottage One, walked past a few clumps of dusty, weary yucca and the three flagpoles cemented into the bed of thriving roses, then stamped the thick dust from my boots on my way across the concrete porch to the big, heavy oak door. My spirits were down as I did a barnyard shuffle on the straw mat to keep from dragging manure inside

Delivered

across the gold and brown tweed carpet.

Manure?

"Well, Johnny Moffitt," I muttered to myself, "at least you ain't what you used to be. Thank God for that!" I wondered how Henry, our one and only resident as far as I knew, was coming along.

I pushed the door open, and scanned the solid birch panelling, the cathedral ceiling, the huge, homey, brown-brick fireplace and hearth.

First class, I thought. *Everything here first class except me.*

I closed the door behind me and threaded my way through the game tables and barrel-back chairs, wondering where I fit into the scene.

Then I saw the boy standing at the far end of the serving counter with his back towards me, fiddling with the spigot to the shiny chrome milk dispenser.

He gave me a start. *Joel?*

No, not Joel. Joel would have been sixteen by now. But the kid was the spitting image of Joel at his age— probably six, probably minus a few front teeth. In his rolled-up blue jeans and baggy tee shirt the boy had the same makings of the athlete that Joel had had at that age, the same straight blond hair with double cowlick. He'd hate that cowlick for the rest of his life.

The boy was muttering, softly blistering the air with an opinion to gladden the heart of a drunk sailor tangling with the Shore Police. But, at the staccato of high heels clicking down the hall in his direction, he quickly shifted gears into poor and pitiful.

"Paaat?" he mourned, "Paaat? Help me, Paaat?"

Housemother Pat Mathis wove her way through her spotless, modern kitchen.

I thought, *What a gal! Now, there's class.*

Tall, straight and pretty with black curls just barely

You sure ain't allowed to cuss!

dancing on her shoulders, Pat swung around the counter, grinned and waved at me, then bent down and hugged the pint-sized con-man. Tilting the big dispenser to get the milk flowing, she called to me over her shoulder, "Hey, Johnny, we've missed you. You've been so busy down at the cow pens, you haven't met our Tommy, here. He's our newest boy. Been with us almost two weeks."

I crossed the room and stuck out my hand. "Hi ya, Tommy."

Tommy blessed me with a toothless, milk-trimmed smile. He said hi, shook my hand, then turned back to the milk machine. "Paaat, can I have some more, pleeese?"

Pat motioned me over to the hearth while she refilled his glass. She gave him a pat, then joined me. "That poor kid," she said. "When he first got here he made me think of a dirty old man in little bitty boys' clothes. You would not believe the words that came out of that rosebud mouth."

"Yes, I would," I said. "I've said them all."

"For the past two years, he's been batted back and forth between children's homes and hospitals. Nobody seemed to be able to work with him, so Child Welfare made application to us. They thought maybe a stable environment with a few brothers would help. Jay and the director brought him from the Children's Psychiatric Hospital in Lubbock."

"How's he get along with Henry?"

"You should have seen them, Johnny," Pat said. "As soon as he walked in here, he and Henry—well, they were brothers at first sight. It doesn't matter to Tommy that Henry is black and fifteen, and it doesn't matter to Henry that Tommy is white and only six."

"Good looking kid," I observed.

"And sharp!" Pat added. "But I don't think he un-

Delivered

derstands the difference between truth and falsehood. He has such a lying tongue, and oh, such a foul mouth! Welfare doesn't tell us these things. And Jay, being slightly hard of hearing, doesn't seem to hear it all."

"How's the kid doing otherwise?"

"Well, I will say at least he's not lazy. Remember how Henry was? He'd been a ward of the State so long, he thought he never had to do anything. But now that Henry and Tommy are sharing a room—well, you know Jay, the proverbial iron fist in the velvet glove. With a little persuasion from him, both boys keep themselves clean and their room picked up. They walk all over me; I'm just a pushover."

"Maybe they need both."

"I'm not so sure about that," she said. "We're still having lots of problems with the local school board. But anyway, about Tommy. Since he had so many major personal problems, Jay decided on the first day to tackle just one at a time. He decided to concentrate first of all on his mouth."

"How did that go?"

"Well, he took Tommy aside, sat down with him and said, 'Tommy, the Bible says that foolishness is bound up in the heart of a child, and the rod of correction drives it far from him. Now, cussing is foolishness. And because God has put me in charge of you, and holds me accountable for what you do, when you cuss, I'm going to spank you. Do you understand?'

"Tommy didn't answer, but who knows what he was thinking. So Jay opened the Bible to Proverbs 22:15, and said, 'Look, Tommy, I want you to see in here what I just told you.'

"Tommy leaned over and stared at the page for a minute, then looked up at Jay, shrugged his shoulders, and said, 'I can't read.' "

You sure ain't allowed to cuss!

I had to laugh.

Pat continued. "Yeah, he's cute, isn't he! Anyway, Jay said, 'Well, I can read, so you can take my word for it.' Then, he took Tommy into his room and spanked him. Tommy screamed like he was being killed, but we expected that.

"When Tommy cussed again later that day, Jay spanked him again, and the next day and the next, every day for the past two weeks, sometimes five and six times in one day: Tommy cusses, Jay spanks. Jay is beginning to wonder if it is doing him any good at all."

My heart was breaking for the kid—unruly, undisciplined, unsure. What I saw in Tommy reminded me of myself at that age—the profanity, the bravado, the swagger. I had been left on my own, but at least now Tommy had somebody who cared paying attention. I lived twenty-seven wasted years before the Lord finally got my attention and showed me that, even if nobody else cared, He did.

I watched Tommy, thinking that at six years old he was old enough to begin taking some responsibility for his own actions, old enough to begin making some firm decisions, old enough to begin understanding his options—to be good or to be bad, to say yes or to say no, to care or not to care—and to anticipate the results of his choices.

When I was six I chose to say no. I chose not to care and nobody stopped me. I wanted to see Tommy stopped, to be turned around before he had to experience a lot of the same mistakes and wasted years that described my life.

Pat's hand on my arm interrupted my thoughts, and she changed the subject. "Johnny, how do you like being farm-ranch director here?"

Delivered

"I don't," I said truthfully, with a tinge of bitterness. "I'm not a farmer; I'm a PR man. My heart is with the program—preaching and teaching and motivating others to action. The Tommys and Henrys are the whys of this place: why the vision, the building, the spiritual growing pains and stretching we're all going through. The boys, not the cows! And I'm beginning to wonder if the operation here is a Christ-centered ministry or a beef business."

Watching Tommy sip his milk and glare at me from the far end of the room, I already knew I was not the one who could really help him. He had too many complex problems—deep problems—and I was not qualified. God knew how much I wanted to help steer him away from gangs, from drugs, from prison. I knew that God was his only hope, the only One qualified to change the direction of his life. And I knew that God's heart was breaking over Tommy, just like it had over me for so many years.

Jay came in, a big happy man, a former pilot. His rugged face was wreathed in smiles. He came in through the front door, crossed the room and introduced his companion, a lanky young reporter for the daily *Lubbock Avalanche Journal*, who was happily scribbling in a spiral notebook about the size of his hand. The reporter was eager to cap his feature article about the new ranch with a statement from one of our two resident boys.

Jay grinned at me, winked at Pat, and scanned the room, probably hoping for Henry. But too late. The reporter spotted Tommy and headed straight for him. Jay braced himself. Pat reached for his hand.

"Hello there, young fellow," the reporter said brightly. "What's your name?"

"Tommy."

The reporter wrote it down.

You sure ain't allowed to cuss!

"You live here, do you?"

Tommy stared.

"Well, Tommy," he said, "how do you like it here?"

Pat repeated the question into Jay's ear. Jay held his breath while Pat chewed her lower lip. Tommy frowned and squirmed, buffing the toe of his gym shoe on the carpet, trying to decide how he liked it at the TBR. It was the first time the question had been put to him. The reporter licked the tip of his pencil and waited.

Finally, Tommy answered. "I'll tell you one thing about this place!" He glanced up at Jay. "You sure ain't allowed to cuss!"

Jay and Pat sighed in relief. The reporter laughed in delight and left happy.

But, as I backed the pickup out of the parking area and headed home, I still nursed my bad attitude.

I've had it around here, I thought. *I'm tired. The best thing for me to do is quit this place. I might as well; I've quit everything else I ever started—school, probably a hundred jobs, the Bandidos . . .*

I parked the truck and got out. Betty's dog Honey waggled up to me and slobbered on my boots. I stared down at her until I finally resolved my decision.

"Nope!" I said out loud to myself, "I won't quit! God gave me this place in a vision. I've worked hard getting it going. Betty and the kids and I are finally living in a nice new home, and I'm not the person I used to be. I'm not going to quit!" And I bounded up the steps.

The Bandidos—I hadn't thought about them for a long time. I knew from my experience with the Bandidos, that gang bikers are not misguided kids being naughty; they are grown men very often being bad. I had heard that Crazy Willie had been killed in a fight, and that Beer Can was serving a life sentence for murder.

Delivered

Betty met me at the door and handed me a letter. Without glancing at the return address, I kept thinking out loud, "Some of the others are probably dead, too; some in prison . . ."

"Who?"

"The Bandits. I was just wondering about Cliff and Catfish. I wonder if Cliff is still riding with the Ghost Riders, and if Catfish made it in the Navy."

"Johnny, you got a letter. I put it in your hand."

"I'd sure like to see old Catfish."

CHAPTER SEVENTEEN

"It says what you said it says."

For my thoughts are not your thoughts, neither are your ways my ways, saith the Lord.   Isaiah 55:8

For thou shalt go to all that I shall send thee, and whatsoever I command thee, thou shalt speak.
Jeremiah 1:7

1975: Lubbock, Plainview

I glanced, then stared, at the return address on the letter. "This is weird, Betty," I said. "This letter is from the director. He's out here every day. I wonder why he's sending me a letter through the mail."

"Open it and see what it says."

I opened it and read it out loud. It said, in effect, that, for failure to comply with his request to complete construction of the working pens by the end of the week, my employment with the Texas Boys Ranch was terminated upon one month's notice.

"What!" I shouted. I couldn't have read it right. "Betty, look at this," I said, shoving the single page into her hand. "What does it say?"

She scanned the letter, and said, "You read it right. It says what you said it says."

I was outraged. Stomping around the room in my dusty boots I shouted, "I gave birth to this place! God gave me the vision for this place! I helped build it with my own hands! This guy is crazy!"

Delivered

"Johnny," Betty said, "are you sure this isn't God? I've been wanting to leave this place ever since we moved in. You're not happy; I'm not happy. I've been crying; you've been crying . . ."

"Betty, let's go over to Plainview this weekend. Let's go somewhere, and pray this through."

"Okay, but first, why don't you try to talk to the director about it? Ask him why he did this to you."

I phoned his house, but he had gone out of town for a week.

On Friday afternoon, we left the boys with Hazel and Joe, drove to Plainview, and checked into a motel. All weekend we read the Bible and prayed and asked God for a word from Him. Over and over He directed our attention to Jeremiah 1:7: *For thou shalt go to all that I shall send thee, and whatsoever I command thee, thou shalt speak.*

On Sunday morning, Betty said, "The only conclusion I can come to, Johnny, is that God has called you to preach, and you're not doing it at the ranch. You're called to minister, not to build cow pens."

"That's fine, Betty, but right now our life is a scrambled-up mess, and what I want to know every day is, where are we going to get supper that night."

"All right, Johnny, why don't we go back and talk to Morris or some other godly man and tell him the situation and ask him what he thinks we should do?"

"We're not going to do that, because we just don't do it that way. There is no man in the world who would take the responsibility of saying to me, 'I think you should quit your job,' or, 'I think you should stay,' or, 'I think this is God's will for you.' Nobody, just nobody is going to give me any cut-and-dried, exact instructions."

"Then let's just go home."

"I am spiritual enough, Betty," I said, "that, if God has anything to tell me, He can tell me without having to speak through some other man."

CHAPTER EIGHTEEN

"It's from God."

Now concerning spiritual gifts, brethren, I would not have you ignorant.   1 Corinthians 12:1

1975: Lubbock

As we pulled out of Plainview onto the freeway, I pointed and said, "Betty, look! There's Calvary Temple where Garry Page is pastor. He was preaching at Trinity Church the night I got saved. Let's catch the service there this morning before we go home."

All that week at Calvary Temple, Hilton Sutton had been teaching a seminar on the manifestation of the gifts of the Holy Spirit. We caught the last session that morning.

At the end of the service, Hilton demonstrated his message literally when he said to me, "Johnny, I have a word of knowledge for you from the Holy Spirit. You are contemplating a change in your ministry, and it's from God."

On Monday morning, I took my letter of dismissal to the chairman of the TBR personnel committee.

"Did you get a copy of this?" I asked him.

"Yes, I did."

"What did you think of it?"

"I didn't know what to think. I was waiting for you to come see me about it."

"All I want," I said to him, "is for him to tear up this letter, and let me resign."

Delivered

"Johnny," he said, "are you sure? You've been under a lot of pressure since we started this project, so don't be hasty. We can fight it, if you want to."

"No, I don't want to cause a split."

"Well, you're right there," he said. "The ranch and the ministry to the boys are more important than any one of us individually. Do you think you got a raw deal?"

"I think it was a rotten way to handle it, but it's done, and I don't have any bitterness about it. This work is God's; the main thing is helping the boys. I've got peace about it."

The letter of dismissal was withdrawn, and I resigned. Betty and I had one month to decide what to do and where to go, so I started checking the ads.

"Betty," I said, "here's an ad for a house for sale. I'm going to see if we can rent it. I'll be back in a little while."

When I returned I said, "Betty, we're going to buy that house. As a matter of fact, we're going to buy two houses—two houses and an apartment . . ."

"What are we going to use for a down-payment, your charm and my beauty?"

". . . two houses, an apartment and a swimming pool. The owners are moving to California and have had it on the market for a long time. The man said he would carry the note at six percent because he's disgusted with the banks and their twelve and thirteen percents, so he's going to carry it at six percent with nothing down . . ."

"I'm glad we don't have to trade our babies."

". . . and he said they've saved up $200 to have the place cleaned up, so if we clean it up, he will give us the $200 in cash. Now listen, for $25,000 with no down-payment we get two acres, a house for us, two rental properties, a swimming pool, and a $200 bonus."

"God's been working overtime."

I grinned. "With God, all-the-time isn't overtime!"

It's from God.

My faith took such a leap that without consulting Betty I decided to buy a new car. Faith? Or presumption? After working a deal trading our two clunkers, I saddled myself with monthly payments of $242 for four years, drove home in a brand new brown Hornet Sportabout and said," Betty, God is going to pay off this new car!"

But God spoke to my heart and said, "No, I'm not. You didn't consult Me on this. You didn't take Me along when you bought it. I didn't sign My name to the note. You are going to pay for it yourself."

And for the next five months I was like a fish flopping in the bottom of the boat. Would I never learn? With no income from the ranch, I installed swimming pools and did maintenance on nursing homes just to keep up with the payments not only on the car, but also on a big television set, while Betty wrapped meat at Scaggs. The neglected, rundown condition of the two houses and the pool and the yard was a sore spot with Betty, but my heart wasn't into repairs and upkeep at home. I was always so tired and frustrated whenever I was home, that I just sank in front of my favorite escape, the television.

Betty worked nights, saw Travis between naps, saw Terry about an hour a day, saw me sleeping or watching TV.

She would walk through the house, muttering, "I hate TV. I hate you. I hate me. I hate life. I hate . . . I hate . . ." Then one night, while she was driving home from work, she said, "God, I don't care what You want anymore. I just want money. This is the first time in my life that I don't care if I'm doing Your will. I want money. I want lots of money. I don't want to live like this anymore. I'll take any moral job that will pay. I just want money."

About a week later, I awoke early one morning. Betty

Delivered

was already up and dressed, getting ready to go out. I rolled over and said, "What time is it?"

"It's quarter to five."

"What are you doing up?"

"Getting ready to go out."

"Where are you going?"

"I'm going to meet a guy."

That brought me fully awake. "What do you mean, going to meet a guy?"

"I'm going to meet a guy who's going to take me on a run to deliver Fritos, and if I like the job, I'm going to take it and I'm going to make $20,000 a year for the next twenty years."

"You are not!"

"I am and good-bye. I'll be back about six o'clock tonight to fix your dinner." And she closed the door behind her.

I sat on the side of the bed with my head in my hands. I said, "God, what's going on? Why can't we get along any better than this? How come I can't make a living for my family?" I went back to sleep and dreamed that Betty had left me.

Hazel came by a few days later to tell us she was disturbed. "I had a dream about Betty," she said. "I don't know what it means, but Betty was standing in the middle of the street with Terry and Travis, and she was crying. Do you all know what it means?"

I looked at Betty, and she started to cry. God was saying to her, "Wait a minute, daughter. Cast down those destructive, vain imaginations. You are right where I want you to be."

Betty went back to Scaggs and never mentioned the job with Fritos again. But I was still nowhere and I didn't know what to do about it.

In December, I went with Con Davis, one of the pas-

It's from God.

tors at Trinity Church, to a week-long Bill Gothard "Basic Youth Conflicts" seminar in Dallas. During the week, Con asked me if I thought I could locate a school in south Dallas for him. He wanted to visit a professor at Christ For the Nations Institute (CFNI).

"Yeah, Con," I said, "I know Dallas pretty well."

At CFNI, while Con talked with his friend, I walked around the campus, ending up at the office of the registrar, who talked to me about the school, and gave me a catalog and some brochures.

At the hotel I said, "Con, I think God wants me to enroll at CFNI."

He chuckled. "I've known that since you first started the Texas Boys Ranch, but the Lord wouldn't let me tell you. He wanted to do it Himself when the time was right."

Back in Lubbock, I raced into the house. "Betty! Betty! God told me a lot of things on this trip! First, he told me to sell the TV."

"That was God, all right!"

"Then He told me He wants me to go to school in Dallas!"

"That was not God! He does not want you to go to school in Dallas because we live in Lubbock and I'm not moving again!"

CHAPTER NINETEEN

"She wanted to tell me about a dream."

I will instruct thee and teach thee in the way which thou shalt go: I will guide thee with mine eye.

Psalm 32:8

1975-1977: Lubbock, Dallas

Betty said, "We just bought some nice furniture and we just bought this house and we know it was from the Lord because we got it with no down payment and almost no monthly payments and we like it here and it's peaceful here and the kids love it here and my mother is here and our families are here and our church is here and everything is wonderful and neat and groovy, and since I've been married to you I've lived in the red house and the little house and the house with the blue carpet and with my folks and out at the ranch and now here and I'm not moving again!"

"Well, I guess you're right."

"And besides that, there is nobody in the whole world we could get to come here and stay in our house and keep the other house and the apartment rented and take care of our furniture and look after our things while we were away."

"Well, you're probably right."

"Now I'm going into my kitchen to cook your dinner so we can eat in our dining room with our children at our own table."

Delivered

The phone rang, and Betty answered it. "Oh, hello," she said. "You did? About us?" Then she looked at me with an expression I couldn't read. "Hmmm," she said. "Hmmm, you don't say? Well, I don't know, but I guess it's because we'll be in school in Dallas. Um hm. Okay, 'bye."

"Who was that?" I asked her.

"A friend of ours from church."

"Well, what was it all about?"

"She wanted to tell me about a dream she had."

"Well, are you going to tell me?"

"Johnny, she said that they have to move and she had a dream about them living here with all our stuff but we were gone but not permanently and it was such a strange dream she wanted to know if we were planning to move for a few months and did I have an interpretation to her dream."

I just grinned at her.

"So what could I say? I said yes."

"Listen, Betty," I said, "I'll just go for the four-week Jan-Term. If I think it's where the Lord wants us to be, you can move down with the kids in February in time for the Spring Term. I'll come back and help you move."

After my first day of classes, I phoned Betty. I said, "Start packing."

"Pack what? You've got our one and only car."

"Borrow Joe's van, and come for a visit. Bring the kids."

I gave her directions and calculated their time of arrival if she didn't get lost. She got lost. She circled the city, drove out to the lake, came back into town, explored the inner city, and was about to head back to Lubbock when she accidently found the school. After two great days, on their way back out of town on Monday morning they had a flat.

She wanted to tell me about a dream.

Our friends from church leased the house. While Betty was packing in Lubbock, I went to the admissions officer at CFNI to tell him I would be gone for the weekend to help my wife pack and move. He said it would cost me $400, my GI benefits for the month, which I would forfeit if I cut the Sunday classes.

Joe and Hazel helped Betty. They borrowed a trailer made from the bed of an old pickup truck, then packed and repacked till midnight. A friend who owned a used-car lot offered Betty the use of an old Dodge that had a trailer hitch, and a young couple we knew agreed to go along to help with the driving.

At ten o'clock Saturday morning, Hazel and Joe waved them all good-bye from the front windows. At ten-thirty, Terry walked back into the house and said, "Are you still crying, Grandma?"

Betty trailed in behind him and said, "We got as far as the first filling station but the bottom of the car was dragging and I knew that by the time we got to Dallas we'd be on fire."

Betty returned the car, and the young couple decided not to go after all. But Joe had a friend who had a heavy-duty station wagon that also had a hitch. After transferring the trailer and furniture and boxes and bags, Joe and Hazel decided to go, too, so Joe could do the driving. The following morning, they piled in with Betty and the boys. Joe shifted into low. As they moved forward, a rear wheel hit a shallow hole in the driveway; the trailer bounced off the hitch, and hit the ground. Joe got out and hitched up again, checking to make sure that this time the lock was properly engaged.

When he climbed back into the driver's seat, Betty said, "Let's pray."

At CFNI, Betty and I both enrolled as students. I not only attended classes, but I also worked for the AA Mo-

Delivered

torcycle Escort Service, escorting trucks and funeral processions through town, and teaching people how to ride motorcycles without getting killed. I also worked part-time in construction, attended church three times a week, and became involved in the school's prison ministry.

Betty attended classes from 8 a.m. until noon, studied sign language from 1:00 till 2:00, retrieved our boys from day-care at 2:30, took voice lessons, was involved in child evangelism, went to church, did all the cooking, cleaning and laundry, and was soon running from room to room because she didn't have time to walk.

A student named Sid Smith and I formed the Rhema Prison Ministry. From material taught by Prof. Carroll Thompson, I drafted a Bible study called the "Doctrinal Foundation Series." I presented it to the chaplain at Seagoville Prison, who immediately said, "Go ahead and use it." For the two years I was at CFNI, I taught weekly Bible studies in the Seagoville Federal Prison and the co-ed federal penitentiary in Fort Worth.

By January 1977, I was convinced that I could bring home more money if I was working for myself. So, with $400 I bought a secondhand, heavy-duty truck, and soon had more hauling and construction job offers than I could accept.

In March, I received my first communication from the Texas Boys Ranch since we had left. It was a letter from the chairman of the board, saying that at a recent meeting a motion was carried and approved unanimously to rename Cottage One, the Johnny Moffitt Cottage. He wanted to know if it met with my approval.

Yeah, it met with my approval, with tears.

A note from Pat Mathis said that Cottage Two, built by the Lubbock Lions Club, was scheduled to open that year. She also quoted part of Tommy's psychiatrist's report: "This can't be the same child," he wrote. "What-

She wanted to tell me about a dream.

ever you are doing, keep it up. If you ever need me again to help with him, just call, but I know you never will."

In May, Trinity Church licensed me as a minister of the gospel.

In the fall, Cookie Rodriguez came from New Life for Girls in Pennsylvania to speak to the students at CFNI. She also visited the jails with us. Then, when she was invited by a group calling themselves Maranatha to hold a two-day crusade the following January in their little Georgia town of Milledgeville, she hired me as her advanceman.

With a singer named Tim I flew to Georgia for ten days to advertise the crusade by showing Cookie's film, "Please Make Me Cry." We showed it thirty-two times in churches, schools, colleges, prisons and youth development centers in and around Milledgeville and Baldwin County. On our first day there, while helping Tim unload his sound equipment, I wrenched my back and could hardly move. But there was no quitting this time. We borrowed a van with a bed, and between meetings I crawled slowly and painfully into the back of the van to lie flat until the muscle-relaxer pills took effect, the same kind of pills I had taken in Puerto Rico and on the breed farm.

At five-thirty in the afternoon before Cookie's first scheduled meeting, she phoned me from Pennsylvania. "Johnny," she rasped over the phone, "I called to let you know that I'm not coming."

CHAPTER TWENTY

"I think God wants us to be involved."

This is the way, walk ye in it.   Isaiah 30:21b

1977-1983: Dallas, Milledgeville

"I'm not coming," Cookie rasped. "I've been preaching too hard, and my doctor won't let me talk. I'm sending my husband Demi in my place."

I stared at the phone in semi-shock. Everybody was primed to hear Cookie, to see the former heroin addict who was touching the lives of so many lost souls across the country. I didn't want to tell them she wasn't coming, but I had no choice.

After two days of powerful ministry by Demi, a member of Maranatha described to me a vision he had about a work in Milledgeville. He wasn't clear on what it was to be; he just knew that God wanted to do something in his hometown.

While there, I introduced a man, who to the best of my knowledge was the oldest prisoner in the United States, to the Lord Jesus Christ. At 92, he was serving time for killing one of a gang of boys he could not see when he tried to scare them off his property with a shotgun blast.

The prisoner was locked up in the Colony Farm Prison in Milledgeville, Georgia, and I was there to preach. But before I started, I sat down next to the old man and said, "Tell me about yourself."

Delivered

For fifteen minutes he poured out his heart to me. When I got up and preached the Word of God and gave the invitation to trust Christ for salvation, he was the first one down to the altar. I glanced over at the chaplain, who was bawling like a baby. It was the first time in over two years that the old man had responded to anyone.

The inmate got parole. He went home a new man, a new creature, a new creation in Christ. He had found the Lord of his life, and I, Johnny Moffitt, an underachiever from the word Go, had fulfilled the ultimate charge entrusted to me. By boldly speaking the eternal truth of the gospel of Jesus Christ to a small congregation of underachievers, I had rerouted a soul headed for hell.

Back home at CFNI, I said, "Betty, this ministry in Georgia—I think God wants us to be involved. It's . . ."

But Betty interrupted me. "Johnny," she said, "in the last three months you thought God wanted us to move to Puerto Rico, God wanted us to move to Mississippi, God wanted us to move to Pennsylvania. You are just trying to quit school before you graduate, and I'm not going to let you do it. We're not leaving. You just so much want to do God's will you jump at everything. One of our professors said that when God is calling us to do something there will be one, two, three, four, five, six, seven, eight things in a row confirming it. I want to be open to the Spirit of God, too, but I'm not ready to fly away and do some dumb thing. And besides, I'm pregnant."

In April, I was invited back to Milledgeville to preach. While I was there a denominational preacher, who had five churches on his circuit, offered me a house in Milledgeville if I would move there and preach for him on Sunday mornings. Maranatha offered to be the tax shelter.

I think God wants us to be involved.

There are five prisons in the small town of Milledgeville, plus the Youth Development Center and a large mental hospital. I had already met most of the prison chaplains while I was there for Cookie. Here was confirmation to satisfy even Betty: a house, support through a denominational church, an organization to work with, and seven mission fields right in town. What more did we need?

All Abraham had was a word from the Lord.

Near the end of April, the student in charge of the CFNI jail ministry knocked on my door. "My name is Duane Bristow," he said, "and God told me to move my family to Milledgeville, Georgia. I've never been there, but I hear you're going, so I thought I'd come over to see if we could talk about it."

"Come on in!"

I had just contracted to begin landscaping and paving a parking lot in Dallas, so I hired Duane to help me build the needed railroad-tie retaining wall for it and to pour concrete. By the time we had poured three 15-yard sections and set sixty cross ties, we knew God wanted us to work together in Milledgeville. We prayed in the truck going to work and we prayed in the truck returning home. On the job we compared jail and prison ministry experiences, and shared about where we were coming from and where we thought we were going. We praised God and made plans, while Betty and Duane's wife Marilyn formed a friendship, and our two boys and their two daughters got acquainted at school.

Just before graduation in May 1979, I sold the old truck. At the same time a friend of ours sold our property in Lubbock for us. Altogether we had enough cash to send in a late-as-usual payment on the brown Hornet, and to rent a truck to haul our furniture to Milledgeville. We even had over $200 to spare.

Delivered

Thanks to Betty's perseverance in tying me down every time I came close to flying away, my making it through the graduation exercises seemed to break my dropout habit. I had started as a two-year student, and in May I had a diploma in my hand to prove that this thirty-five-year-old nonachiever could achieve.

The possessions we couldn't stuff into the rented truck got packed around Marilyn and the girls in the Bristows' car and around Betty and the boys in the Hornet. Duane and I piled into the truck and we headed east to Milledgeville. I thought of Stanley and Sue. It had been four years since Betty and I had seen them or even talked to them. We were surprised to find Sue quite pregnant with Misty, who would be born in June, as was Betty with our baby due in August.

Stanley and Sue were satisfied with their life of work and booze, so they said. They were not interested in the gospel. So the first goal we set when we left Texas was seeing them saved.

We pulled into Milledgeville on the third day at ten o'clock at night, confident that we had arrived at the right place at the right time on God's perfect timetable. The next morning, however, we discovered that only one item on our long list of confirmations still stood firm: The mission fields were still there.

"Johnny," Betty said, "you might just as well have moved me to China because all these trees and bushes give me claustrophobia and there aren't any street lights and the roads are not like Texas and the land is not like Texas and the people don't talk like Texans and nothing is like Texas and nothing is working out and everybody is out of town and nobody can tell us anything and this place is kudzu-city!"

"Betty," I said, "God did not send me halfway across the United States to pour concrete. We're going to stay

I think God wants us to be involved.

here in middle Georgia and minister through whatever door He opens. Joe sent us some money, and I'm going out to rent us a house."

"What are we going to do for furniture? We don't have enough."

"What do we need?"

"A dinette set and a dresser and a big chair and a refrigerator and a stove and a washing machine—for starters."

I found us a house. The landlady said, "I need to leave some furniture in there. I hope it's all right with you."

"What kind of furniture?"

"A washing machine, a stove, a refrigerator, a reclining chair, a dresser and a dinette set."

"That'll be just fine!"

Duane and I called an organizational meeting with Maranatha and some of the other men from town, to share with them what we wanted to do. We told them we had a message to underachievers and, as we saw it, the most concentrated group of underachievers in the world could be found in the prisons. We wanted to tell them that Jesus Christ is in the life-changing business, changing underachievers into achievers.

We wanted to tell them that, when Jesus told Peter and Andrew, "Follow Me and I will make you to become fishers of men," the emphasis was on "make you to become." Peter and Andrew were already fishermen. If they had been carpenters or bricklayers, He probably would have said, "I will make you to become builders of the Heavenly Kingdom." If they had been bikers, He would have said, "I will make you to become messengers of My Word." We wanted to tell them that Jesus takes men right where they are, men who seem worthless, and makes them into men who are worthwhile, and that no-

Delivered

body is beyond that potential.

The men at that meeting were interested and they asked questions:

Q. "Do you honestly believe that men can change?"

A. "I'm walking proof of the fact that they can."

Q. "What is your basic message?"

A. "That they don't have to counteract their poor self-image with the Big Life Lie that they are 'cool,' but that they are worth loving, and that somebody cares. That they are responsible for their own actions. That somebody along the line said, 'Let's do this,' and they said okay when they should have said no. And that right now they need to get saved and filled with the Holy Spirit."

Q. "Where do you start?"

A. "By getting them off the thought of getting out. Get their minds on the thought of changing not their locations but their lives, and then let God get them out. Some of them are so busy playing the game they think will get them out, that they can't separate reality from fiction anymore. They can talk the God-talk with Oral Roberts or Billy Graham, but they don't know Jesus from apple-butter. Even if they work the game and do get out, they won't stay out.

"Everything we do," I said, "is geared to getting that man to change his thinking about himself, to change his inner life—a metamorphosis from caterpillar to butterfly—a new creation. And since the new creature is totally alien to the old, he needs to be taught again how to eat and sleep, talk and crawl, and walk and live."

Q. "What's your program?"

A. "We have evangelistic meetings followed up by Bible studies, weekly wherever possible. We teach our 'Doctrinal Foundation Series' until we are satisfied that they are grounded in the Word of God. Then we start building on that. We know the general direction each

I think God wants us to be involved.

session will go, but we are always open to the redirection of the Holy Spirit.

"Sometimes we preach; sometimes we take guest speakers or musicians. We especially want the pastors of the churches that support the ministry to go in and get the feel of it—all the Christian denominations, whoever wants to go. Then, when the men are released, we stay with them as much as they want to stay with us."

Q. "Aren't you afraid?"

A. "If God is not leading me to go in there, I have no business going. If He is, I am as safe in prison as I am in my own bed."

Q. "What do you do about con men?"

A. "Deal with them on that basis. I tell them, 'I believe you are playing games with me!'"

Q. "How do you feel about capital punishment?"

A. "That is no deterrent to sin. Only Jesus Christ is."

Q. "How far does your help go?"

A. "Our help goes as far as their criminal case."

At the end of the meeting, we formed a new nonprofit corporation, a new "A Voice in the Wilderness." Duane and I then began in earnest to call on the prison chaplains in the area. We invited them to lunch; they in turn invited us to their prisons.

All this activity was encouraging, but I still needed specific confirmation from God that our vision was His vision. Then, Bill Goins, director of prison chaplains of the state of Georgia, held a one-day workshop for chaplains at the Women's Prison in Milledgeville, and we went. At the luncheon, Gene Bartholf, Chaplain of the Macon Correctional Center, was sitting to my left, while his father Harry, Chaplain of Georgia State Prison at Reidsville, was to my right.

Harry spoke across me to his son, and said, "Gene, I just got through listening to a tape I found in the Geor-

Delivered

gia State Prison library, about an ex-motorcycle rider from Texas, who got saved, and started a prison ministry with another guy in Dallas. They call it 'Rhema Prison Ministry.' A powerful testimony. I want you to hear it."

"Excuse me," I said, "but what's the guy's name?"

"Johnny Moffitt."

"That's me."

"What?"

"I'm Johnny Moffitt."

"Well, great!" Harry said. "Glad to have you in Georgia. Everything in Reidsville is closed right now because of the riots there—one guard and six inmates killed, and the Muslims tried to burn down the chapel. No meetings of any kind—no movies, no chapel services, nothing. But as soon as they open up again, I want you to come on down there and preach."

That's the kind of confirmation I was looking for.

When I finally made the last payment on the Hornet after only 50,000 miles, the differential was shot, the brakes were shot, the tires were shot, the shocks were shot—everything was shot. But a brother with a used-car lot took it off my hands and traded me even for an old blue station wagon. It had been a hard lesson. But God was blessing in other ways, especially in August when He gave us our beautiful baby daughter whom we named Emily.

One day, I said to Duane, "Let's sponsor a prison-ministry conference. There's no place for us to go to learn how to do this work, and ministers need to share with one another what's working for them and what's not, like a trade show for prison ministers."

Duane said, "Sounds good to me."

As a result of that conversation, in January 1979, we ventured a trial, three-day "First Annual Prison Ministry Conference," sponsored by AVIW and held in the

I think God wants us to be involved.

Baldwin County Community Center in Milledgeville. We had six speakers with 100 in attendance.

In January 1980, our "Second Annual Conference" attracted over 200 prison ministers, volunteers and supporters to Milledgeville from across the country and from all walks of life—educational, social, denominational and financial. They came needing information, instruction and support, and parted having committed themselves to helping each other with resources, follow-up, and new doors of ministry.

God was confirming the vision.

Somewhat akin to Jack's magic bean, the idea quickly sprouted. By 1983, it had grown into a trans-denominational, international network we called the Coalition of Prison Evangelists, or COPE. The core group consisted of:

President Frank Costantino, Christian Prison Ministries and The Bridge Aftercare Center, Orlando, Florida (ex-convict);

Vice President Johnny Moffitt, A Voice in the Wilderness Prison Ministry, Milledgeville, Georgia (ex-biker); and

Secretary/Treasurer Karen Nelson, Nelson Ministries, Jonesboro, Georgia (evangelist, wife and mother).

Also Bobby Henderson, Fellowship Mission, Shreveport, Louisiana (ex-convict, former alcoholic);

Jeff Park, PTL Prison Ministry, Fort Mill, South Carolina (radical hippie in the '60s);

Jim Black, Faith Prison Ministries (ex-convict);

Tony Satriano, Lovelight Ministries, Dallas, Texas (former body guard on the fringes of the underworld);

Fernie Mancillas, New Life Prison Ministries (ex-convict).

The first COPE Conference was held in May 1983, in Atlanta's Quality Inn, with three of the most experienced

Delivered

and foremost leaders in prison evangelism addressing the conference. They were Chaplain Ray Hoekstra, Rev. Bill Glass, and Paul Markstrom. The more than 300 in attendance came from 29 states nationwide. Many had never been in prison ministry, but had come to learn how to get started.

In the wake of that conference came the first, weeklong COPE in-prison revival held at Attica (New York) State Prison in October 1984. While there, I inquired about Philip Debula, an inmate who had made a commitment to Jesus Christ in one of my meetings there in 1980. Nobody knew his whereabouts. Regardless, miracles took place that only God's Spirit could achieve.

During one session, the Lord brought a supernatural word of knowledge through me that two men were on the verge of suicide, but that God wanted to deliver them. The two men confessed, and both surrendered their lives to Christ.

I recalled how by the mercy of God a word of knowledge had instantly delivered me a few years earlier from the crippling fear of my former friends and enemies, the Bandidos. I thanked God in my heart for the supernatural gifts of the Holy Spirit.

During another session, a Muslim leader declared that he wanted to change his personal identification card to Christian. Only God could do that.

The COPE core group grew rapidly. We formed an executive board, incorporated, and set policy, disciplines and goals. We issued ID cards, a membership list, a newsletter, and other published materials, plus consulting assistance from the officers, and full voting privileges—like the Bandidos Brotherhood, but with opposite standards and benefits.

Our published materials consisted primarily of *The Crime Fighter*, written by Frank Costantino, and *The Prison*

I think God wants us to be involved.

Ministry Resource Manual, edited by Jeff Park.

"We covenanted our labor to produce an image of prison ministry through COPE that is worthy of the name of Jesus" (from COPE Goals and Standards).

Norman Carlson, Director of the Federal Bureau of Prisons, writes: "No prison can change a man; change must come from the heart."

We knew that. Rehabilitation is not what we want to see in prisons because to rehabilitate is to restore a person to his former condition, that which made the prisoner a liar, cheat, thief, murderer or rapist in the first place.

In the same vein, educate a criminal and you end up with an educated criminal.

Knowing God is the power to a changed life.

CHAPTER TWENTY-ONE

"Did you call me for money?"

Is it not to deal thy bread to the hungry, and that thou bring the poor that are cast out to thy house; when thou seest the naked, that thou cover him; and that thou hide not thyself from thine own flesh?
Isaiah 58:7

1985-1989: Eatonton

From the time we left Dallas in 1978, our set goal was to see Stanley and Sue saved. They were continually on our minds and in our prayers. Everywhere I spoke, I asked the people to pray for them. Shortly after we visited them on our way to Georgia, they moved from Buffalo Gap to Grand Isle at the southernmost tip of Louisiana, to manage apartments and a motel. Stanley's beauty-contest trophies at final count numbered 52, and by then he was tired of the beauty business.

In Grand Isle, he and Sue were bootlegging fish— buying redfish and speckled trout from the crew members on Florida-owned, commercial-boats, before the catch was counted and delivered to the designated markets. Stanley would then process the bootlegged fish and resell them to local restaurants. Stanley always carried a lot of cash, so he also carried a gun, just like I had for so long.

I was surprised that they moved so far from Fort

Delivered

Worth and Stanquinta, Stanley's oldest daughter by his first wife and mother of his first grandchild.

Stanley and Sue liked their life of work, booze and fishing rodeos, so they said, and were still not interested in the gospel. But Stanley was never off my mind. Whenever I telephoned him, if he was offshore fishing, he would always call me back.

"What's on your mind, Johnny?"

"Stanley, God is wanting to be working in your life."

"Man, don't be calling me telling me that stuff. What do you want, Johnny? I ain't got no money. Did you call me for money?"

"No, God is wanting to work in your life."

He would hang up, but then he'd call me back. He'd say, "Are you all right?"

I'd say, "Yeah."

He'd say, "Are you sure, Johnny? I know something's wrong. You been on my mind."

I'd say, "No, Stanley. That's God wanting to work in your life."

He'd say, "Forgit it! Just forgit it!" and he'd hang up on me again.

Remembering how I always reacted when he used to say, "Johnny, get up. Johnny, get a job. Johnny, get settled somewhere," I understood how he felt only too well.

But, when he called me in February 1987, his voice was trembling. "Johnny, Stanquinta's been killed. When they told me, you were the first one come to my mind."

I was horrified. "Stanley, no! What happened?"

He told me that Stanquinta had left her husband Monty in Fort Worth and moved in with her mother and sister in Mineral Wells, bringing their baby with her. She had sued for divorce. Monty followed her, and said he

Did you call me for money?

wanted to talk. He then drove her and the baby to a church-house parking lot, where she was shot in the head. He then rushed her to the hospital claiming it was suicide. But, since she was right-handed and was shot through the left temple, nobody believed him.

Over the phone Stanley said, "Johnny, them Texas police won't touch him. They don't prosecute one drug addict, who's supposed to have killed another addict, and who don't live in their county. I'm on my way to kill him."

I yelled over the phone, "Stanley, wait! Stay there! I'm coming out on the next plane."

"No!" he shouted. "Don't come! I won't be here!"

Inconsolable, Stanley did not cry; he planned revenge instead. I hated leaving him there like that, but I didn't know what else to do.

Stanley tried for six months, but for some reason his truck kept dying, and he couldn't get to the guy. Sue, meanwhile, was in another part of Louisiana, wondering if she would have to get Stanley out of a jail, prison, hospital or morgue.

Frustrated out of his mind, Stanley finally cried out to God. In response, God commanded Stanley to take the gallon of booze he kept in his truck, and pour it out on the ground. Stanley obeyed, and God delivered him instantly from the desire to drink.

Confused and bewildered by what God had done in his life, Stanley came to Georgia, and stayed alone in our house in Eatonton, since Betty and I were out of town. We had no TV hookup, but we did have a video player, so Stanley spent his time watching a this-is-your-life video by ex-convict, prison evangelist Frank Costantino. Stanley returned home impressed with Frank's testimony—and scared.

Delivered

When Sue came home, Stanley told her they were moving east to spend time with Frank. Sue said, somehow she already knew it.

When I counseled with Sue in our Eatonton home one morning, she told me that ever since Joel's funeral many people had tried to talk to her about the Lord. She pretended not to be listening, but thought about Him all the time, daily praying for strength.

Because of something a preacher in Dallas had said to her, Sue had been drinking and crying, blaming God for Joel's death, drinking to hide the pain and hatred she had for the driver. When she finally could accept that God really loved her, she gave up the booze. She eventually forgave both man and preacher, and gave her heart back to Jesus.

That same afternoon I went to see Stanley. I said, "Wanta get saved?"

"Sure, I guess so," he said.

I said, "That's good, 'cause Sue just got saved this morning."

Duane and Marilyn Bristow, our cofounders of AVIW in Georgia, had already gone with another ministry. So while Betty and I traveled, Stanley and Sue occupied our Eatonton house while Stanley worked in Milledgeville helping parolees, men on work release, needy men sent from local churches, and people off the street to build the Prisoner Restoration Center, or PRC. It was another miracle.

Stanley said, "Johnny, God showed me something right off the git-go. The people He puts in your life are people you would never choose to associate with in your former life."

"Is that right? How's that?"

"Well, take you and me, for instance. In my former life you would be the last person in this world I'd choose

Did you call me for money?

to associate with. I always figured that whatever you was into was stupid, odd and weird, and you must be in it for the money. Me? I never did anything unless I had a reason. If I couldn't see it, I didn't believe it. If I saw and wanted something, I'd go after it, it didn't matter what I had to do or who got hurt. I ain't like that anymore."

Later, our board of directors decided that Stanley and Sue should go to Bible school.

"I ain't going to no Bible school," Stanley declared.

"How about you going down to Dunklin with Mickey Evans?" I suggested.

"Yeah," he said, "that's what God is wanting me to do." He was sure of it. He was impressed with Mickey, the "cowboy" in Indiantown, in south Florida, who ran the Dunklin Memorial Camp for drug and alcohol rehabilitation and ministry-training for tough men with tough problems.

At Dunklin, Stanley worked with the cattle, calves and pigs, took ministry training, attended rehab sessions, and went to staff meetings, prisons, and overcomer groups. Even though God was working in his life, he still wanted to kill his son-in-law, and it bothered him.

"Johnny, how could He take away my desire to drink before I even knew Him, and not take away my desire to kill the guy?"

"I don't know," I said. "What's God saying to you about it?"

"He's saying 'Forgive him, and give him over to Me.'"

"Then, that's what you got to do."

Later he said, "Johnny, I ain't going nowhere with my ministry. What's the matter with me?"

"Have you forgiven the guy?"

"No, man. It's impossible!"

Delivered

"What's God saying to you about it?"

When Stanley finally couldn't stand it any longer, he cried out to God and forgave the guy, and his peace was restored. One day, Stanley said, "Johnny, I never knowed I was an alcoholic till God showed me. I figured if you never killed a child, never got arrested for DWI, and didn't drink cheap booze, you was drinking just 'cause you liked it. But I was just like Daddy, couldn't help myself till God took it out of my life."

It was good for Stanley and me to have been apart while he was in Dunklin and I was traveling. We were both changing, both learning from God, and now God was bringing us together, bringing our families together, giving us new vision, a new ministry together.

Recently, Betty asked Stanley, "Now that you've been in the ministry for a few years, what's the one thing about it that really stands out in your mind?"

"That's easy," Stanley said. "Man, no matter where we go, or what city we're in, or who Johnny introduces me to, the first thing they always say is, "So you're Stanley? Well, praise the Lord! We've been praying for you. I'm glad to hear you finally got saved!"

CHAPTER TWENTY-TWO

"Estonia is where I want to be involved."

"Come over and help us." Acts 16:9

1990-1992: Milledgeville, Canada, Russia, Estonia

The COPE core group expanded rapidly after our first conference, and our first taste of international prison ministry came in early 1990.

Frank Costantino, an Episcopal deacon, had earlier arranged an exchange program through the Church of England in which Englishman Ian Ferguson, a prison chaplain from Stratford in northern England, came to Florida and served as chaplain at Raiford Prison, and a Florida chaplain flew to England and served a term in Stratford.

When Frank met Ian in Florida, Ian invited Frank back to England. He went taking some of his books with him, and returned home with an open-door invitation to COPE.

Later in the spring, Betty and I had our own first taste of international ministry when we went with four COPE volunteers to England, where we found great spiritual hunger among the entire chaplaincy. The basic structure is Church of England, and the chaplains we met, all very much in tune with God, very strong in love, concern and caring, were hungry for something spiritual, wonderful and permanent to happen in their prisons.

The major differences I noticed there were twofold:

Delivered

First, England was years behind America in prison construction. Second, they were years ahead of us in the quality of their correction officers who were trained counselors paid in the upper middle-class wage-scale. One female guard in the women's prison in London, for example, was a trained nurse, who had changed her vocation because guard pay was so much higher.

David Sansome, a prison minister with Victory Outreach, reported being so overwhelmed by requests for ministry that he couldn't handle them all. And Bible school students from Africa, Europe, Latin and South America pleaded with us to come or send someone to their countries. The obvious need was overwhelming.

We visited eleven of Her Majesty's Prisons, including one in continual use since 1610. Many of the inmates had never heard the gospel before.

Back home, by midsummer we had held successful regional COPE conferences in New England and the southeast, plus successful revivals in Illinois, Indiana, Texas and Colorado. Membership had more than quadrupled. Every month COPE had been sponsoring crusades and services in prisons across America—thirteen in September 1990 alone. Volunteers ate with the inmates and visited in the yards. Many prisoners came to our services who had never been in a chapel before. One of our main goals was, and still is, to gather the committed Christian inmates together, and teach them how to be a church, to love and encourage each other.

In the fall of 1990, one volunteer and four COPE board members went to Argentina, where they found conditions at Almos Prison near Buenos Aries astounding. In a 1983 prison riot, every window on the five stories had been smashed. An Argentine pastor, under conviction of God's Spirit, had voluntarily moved into the horrendous conditions of the prison, and lived among

Estonia is where I want to be involved.

the men, winning hundreds to Christ. When our people arrived, about 400 inmates were already on their knees in the huge hall praying and worshipping God. After the service, so many men stood to dedicate their lives to Christ, there was no room to bring them all to the altar. The COPE people were grateful to God and our supporters that they had been able to bring cases of Spanish Bibles, correspondence lessons and testimony books to distribute to the new believers—a powerful beginning to our first countrywide crusade in Argentina.

Then, on a cold, windy day that fall, while I was ministering at the Federal Correctional Institution in Lancaster, Massachusetts, my path once again crossed that of Philip Debula. He was there, not as an inmate, but as one of the chaplains of the prison. Philip has become to me a symbol of what God has called me to: not only to bear fruit, but to see that the fruit remain. Someone had watered a seed I planted long ago, and God had given the increase.

In 1990 alone, Betty and I traveled to eighteen states and three foreign countries—England, Canada and Israel. Our "New Beginnings" correspondence course was translated into Spanish. Four new Bible studies were established in Georgia prisons, our first in-prison "Overcomers" group had started, as had our first in-prison marriage-enrichment seminar.

Meanwhile, Terry, our apprentice chef and the oldest of our three children, graduated from college; Travis, our saxophonist, graduated from high school and began preparing for youth ministry; and Emily was learning to play the piano by ear, and had became involved in worship-dancing. Betty was running the AVIW office, teaching a young girls' class at one church, leading worship at another, traveling with me, and sometimes clean-

Delivered

ing house and planting flowers.

In early 1991, we received an invitation from Chaplain Monty Lewis (ex-convict), a member of the Canadian Federal Chaplaincy Committee for the entire nation though strongest where Monty is stationed in New Brunswick in the Maritimes. I went gladly, basically doing the same things there as we had in England, visiting prisons and setting up a schedule to train volunteers.

In March, during a COPE revival at the Federal Correction Institution in Fort Worth, I spotted the president of the Bandidos strolling across the prison yard. I was able to share not only my faith with him, but understanding and friendship as well. As a result he came to the services. I believe God opened that door, and who can foretell the results of that encounter?

While we were still centered in Georgia, the most exciting thing that happened internationally was the collapse of communism, with its promise of open doors throughout Europe.

Meanwhile, a friend in Florida, Dr. Larry Kennedy, administrator of a large Christian foundation, had written the book, *QUALITY LEADERSHIP IN THE NON-PROFIT WORLD*. With connections in Russia, he invited Frank Costantino, Mickey Evans from Dunklin, Florida Prison Warden David Farcas, and me to go with him to St. Petersburg in early 1992. We were thrilled!

While there, the same things happened there as had happened in England and Canada, but the polarization was clearer: In Russia their so-called "free-world culture" was 180° opposite to that of America. It was exactly like entering an impoverished Third World Country. The word that kept coming to my mind was disrepair. Everything was in disrepair—all the equipment, the automobiles, the streets, the buildings—everything gave the appearance of a desperately stricken nation in total dis-

Estonia is where I want to be involved.

repair. In very fact, that's what it was. In America we were always given the impression that Russia was our formidable, strong enemy. But we saw with our own eyes that the entire country was in dire straits. But, strange as it seemed, going into the prisons was just like going into the prisons in Georgia USA.

The hospital we visited was one of only two, very poor, very needy, ill-equipped, devastated, and we spent only a little time there. All the soap and hand-lotion and toothpaste and other supplies we took with us soon disappeared into outstretched hands.

Our specific mission was to Colony Prison. After Dr. Kennedy spoke to the deputy-warden, we went inside, toured the buildings, and took pictures, surprised to see the convicts building a very ornate, unexpectedly small stone "cathedral" with an "onion" on top, inside the prison yard. An Orthodox priest had worked it out with the government for the prisoners to provide the labor.

Afterwards, we went down to Moscow, to visit the prisons there, and that's where I learned why such a tiny church structure in the prison in St. Petersburg. The most photographed building in Russia is St. Basil's Cathedral in Red Square. Unless one knows better, it is easy to think that all those onion tops comprise one church. Not so! Each "onion" tops its own separate church, but all are within one building. One church may not be as large as 12 x 12', but there might be eight crammed into one building. We saw no pews, no statues, only icons and the crypts of the royal tsars. Like so much else in Russia, St. Basil's was not what it appeared to be on the outside, certainly not the American concept of a church.

After we returned home from that first trip into a foreign country, I knew without doubt that God wanted me somehow involved—not to live there, or even to make Russia #1 on my agenda. Just involved, and He

Delivered

would show me how to flesh it out.

Long before communism fell, an Estonian pastor in Canada had returned to Estonia to pioneer underground churches. When Estonia declared itself a free nation, the pastor already had a church, a Bible school, and a working relationship with the Secretary of the Interior who was over the prison system. And he invited Frank to come over and take a look.

Frank went, then came back saying, "Estonia is where I want to be involved."

Not long afterwards, at a COPE board meeting, the possibility of purchasing a fifty-bed hospital to place inside a prison in Estonia for $20,000 was presented to us on video. While we watched and listened, the Lord spoke to me and said, "I want you to buy it."

We discussed it, agreed to go for it, and advertised the project. The money came in, and we bought the hospital. It was as simple as that.

But then, with God all things are possible.

CHAPTER TWENTY-THREE

"We had to have official government contacts."

Let all things be done decently and in order.
1 Corinthians 14:40

1992: Jamaica

It amazed us to see how God worked, drawing these relationships together, using those contacts to expand and stretch us in directions we could never have imagined on our own.

During our years spent in Georgia, a church was raised up out of our ministry, and among the church members was a young man named Steve, who eventually moved with his wife to Jamaica to work with the CFNI school in Montego Bay.

In early 1992, I received a letter from Steve who had met an ex-offender with a vision for prison ministry in Jamaica, and a burning desire to see something happen there on a major scale. They needed help. Would I come?

I had already discovered through my limited international ministry in Russia and Canada that to accomplish much internationally, we had to have official government contacts. We could do almost nothing just because an ex-offender or pastor wanted us to. So I wrote him back.

"I will come . . . on one condition, that he first arrange an appointment for me with a government offi-

Delivered

cial who can tell me something about the prisons there, and who has the authority to open the doors."

Almost immediately the reply came. First, they wanted me to teach at CFNI-Montego Bay for a week. Second, the ex-offender, Jerrod, had arranged an appointment for me with the Secretary of Corrections in Kingston.

Excited about the prospects, Betty and I flew down, I taught my week at CFNI and Betty sang, then we took a little vacation, but I spent most of my time talking with Jerrod, a prime candidate for COPE membership, a guy who spent over sixteen years in the penitentiary on murder charges, who had become a strong Christian, and who now nurtured a healthy personal relationship with the Governor General of Jamaica (the "king" who was appointed for life by the reigning Parliament, a figurehead but with authority, and who lives in the king's house). The Governor General was a strong, spiritual Christian leader. Commissioner Jerrod had arranged an appointment for me with Mr. Knight, Parliamentary Secretary for Corrections.

On the appointed day, I went early to keep my 15-minute appointment at the Parliament House with Mr. Knight, who was 1 1/2 hours late. When he came in, he sat down behind his desk, and said, "What are you doing here?"

I shrugged. "I really don't know," I said. "I got this letter, and came to talk to you about your prisons. Is there any need for me to come back?"

He stood up and said, "Come with me." He took me around the corner into the office of Jamaica's newly-elected Prime Minister, T. J. Patterson, also a fine Christian man. For the next hour, I talked with Prime Minister Patterson, who then sent for Mr. Young, the Minister of Finances, and the three of us chatted about prisons

We had to have official government contracts.

for another hour. Finally, Prime Minister Patterson stood up, then invited me to come back again to Jamaica to minister in the prisons. My 15-minute appointment had lasted over 3 1/2 hours.

Betty and I returned home, set up a new schedule, then went back to Jamaica, being met at the airport by Jerrod and ten pastors who were ready to "do something" in the prisons but not knowing what or how. At the time, a Mr. Maddox was the national chaplain for Jamaica (the only chaplain). We would be happy to share with them what worked for us.

As Betty and I visited the Women's Prison in Fort Augusta, Gun-Court, General Penitentiary, I was struck by both the spiritual and physical needs of those prisons. I wanted to make a strong statement somehow, that God could change their miserable conditions—a big, undeniable statement. The needs were horrendous: men with no clothes, boys with no shoes, all of them with no hygienic products: no soap, no shampoo, no toothpaste, no toothbrushes, no deodorant, nothing of that nature, only toilet paper—usually.

Silently, I prayed, *God, how can I make a statement here that with You all things are possible?*

Inside the dilapidated, rundown General Penitentiary, to the left of the entrance into the first yard and up to the second floor, we saw an old weathered door with metal signs nailed on it like an old shack down in America's Deep South, and two big 1 x 10's crisscrossed over it with a faded, worn-out sign designating "Chaplain's Office."

I said, "Warden, I want to take a picture of that door."

But he stopped me saying, "You can't take a picture of anything in here."

Then I told him, "We're going to reopen that door."

Delivered

"Why would you want to do that!" he said. "That's nothing but a store room."

But I said, "No, you misunderstand me; I'm talking figuratively. We're going to reopen that chaplain's office door!"

At the far end of the building were the ruins of the original chapel that was destroyed in a hurricane in 1907, and never rebuilt—a windowless shell, with a fallen-down piece of metal for a platform, a desecrated brick and crumbled plaster building where the inmates attended church. (I took pictures). In that dump while we held a service with me preaching and Betty singing, God spoke to me: "Here's your statement: Rebuild this chapel."

After some discussion with the warden, we finally entered into an agreement that we would supply the money needed if he would supply the labor—a joint venture to rebuild the church. (They soon began work on it, and, among other things, we shipped them an electric concrete drill and bit, a gift from one of our donors, so they could rewire behind the walls.)

At that time, we also visited the prison hospital with its 35 beds, and a man on every bed lying on a filthy, bare mattress. One man had a raw bullet hole in his leg. Another, whose wife had smuggled heroin into his mouth in a balloon which he had accidently swallowed, lay there struggling for his life. Guys were dying without treatment—no medicines, no bandages, no linens, no blankets—in the sweltering heat without air conditioners. A doctor came by once every week or so. A dentist—well, the dental chair was something out of ancient history.

Appalled by the conditions I said, "Let me tell you what COPE is all about. COPE is about the strong helping the weak. We're coming to Jamaica not to own any-

We had to have official government contracts.

thing, but to build your prison ministry. And, when we've got you good and strong, you know what you're going to have to do? Some other country, maybe Cuba, is going to open up, and you're going to go build that ministry. Everything COPE accomplishes is through joint ventures with other prison ministries. When we joint-venture with other organizations, we are then much more productive and much more economical."

COPE formed a corporation for ministry there, then made a commitment with them to furnish hospital supplies including an ambulance for taking the critically stabbed, wounded and dying out of the prison to a hospital in town. So many needs! They desperately needed uniforms for the prisoners. Only recently had they been able to put the guards into uniform, to tell the guards apart from the convicts.

The Gun-Court Prison in Jamaica, built for people who commit crimes with guns, is where they hold hearings and trials. With no bail or jail system in Jamaica, when a man gets arrested, he's put in that prison to await trial, where the cells are about 5' x 7' with three men to a cell. With two bunk beds and a pallet floor slid under the bunks during the daytime, the cells have no toilets. Prisoners use honey-buckets with an open sewage line running through the center of the camp.

The women's prison is no better, located in an old abandoned 1700's Spanish fort set on the ocean shore, with rusted cannons all around it. The women are all poor. If they have babies, the babies stay in prison with them. We saw some very forlorn women making little cloth shoes for their children. Of the sixty or so Americans in the Jamaican Prison system, the seven or eight who are women are discriminated against and treated shabbily.

Since our first trip over, we have returned and vis-

Delivered

ited the Jamaican prisons several times. Whenever we show up, the prisoners mob us for soap and shampoo, but especially for the Bibles. The International Bible Society makes wonderful, inexpensive, prison-issue Bibles with study helps, so that's what we take. And, of course, we take hundreds and hundreds and hundreds of individual bars of soap, and give every prisoner we see a bar of soap, a toothbrush, a bottle of shampoo, and for the ladies baby oils, hand lotion, and for the Americans sunscreen because their skin is just blistered. And we take socks. For the kids (prison is also for boys age 6-14), athletic equipment, and tennis shoes that our volunteers buy by the dozens at sales. One problem is that so many kids, even 12-year-olds, have big wide 12-EEE feet. We took a lot of footballs, soccer balls, basketballs, and always more socks, and more hygiene products. Upon returning home, I renew my prayer for good, strong, sturdy uniforms for all the prisoners.

On every trip over, we visit with the Governor General, pray for him, and talk about his country. Recently, he held a state dinner meeting for us in his home with fifty Jamaican business leaders. I had brought three American business leaders along to talk about what could be done for their prisons nationwide. I reiterated for them all the things I had explained to the pastors about COPE—that it was about the strong helping the weak—and about the success of joint ventures. I reassured them that we Americans had not come to bail them out of their problems, but to show them the direction they could go. As soon as their prison ministry was strong and productive, we wanted them to do the same thing in another nation.

CHAPTER TWENTY-FOUR

"What was your name in the club?"

With God all things are possible.   Matthew 19:26

1992: Dallas

By the spring of 1992, Betty and I both knew that God was leading us back to Dallas. When I told Stanley, I asked him if he and Sue were ready to take over running the Milledgeville AVIW office.

He said, "No, Johnny Wade. That's not what God is saying to us. You got others that can do that. God wants us workin' with the Salvation Army."

"You sure?"

"If I can't hear directly from God by now, I ain't never gonna hear. And that's what He wants us to do."

Our move back to Dallas triggered scary memories that now made us laugh—all the "confirmations" that fell through, Betty's acute claustrophobia from being surrounded by bushes and trees.

After we settled into our new home in Dallas, one of our first priorities was to file for authorization to do business in Texas as AVIW, our Georgia corporation. But we found out that for many years, there had been a ministry in the state called The Voice in the Wilderness, so we could not file under our old name, which was too close to theirs.

What to do? Since we had too many years invested in the name to change it completely, we called the Board together, read through all our publications, studied our logo, and prayed about our focus. By then, we were already strongly established in Estonia, Belarus, Canada, England, and Jamaica, so the natural thing to do was just add the word Worldwide. With that settled, we simply established a new corporation calling it Worldwide Voice in the Wilderness.

During our expansion into other nations, I never encountered any real difficulty using an interpreter, because at CFNI we had taken a class in cross-cultural communication. The main problem for me was caused by my background and preaching style. I use lots of colloquialisms and idioms that don't translate literally. I use a lot of humor that doesn't translate culturally. My biggest problem was in England, where I thought we spoke the same language. I had no problem in either Jamaica or Canada. But at first, Russia gave me fits, where the interpreter would sometimes just look at me blankly. I could almost hear her thinking, "Huh?" I had to learn to think and speak basic English and talk slowly, preaching one-point instead of six-point sermons. I have tried to cut my sermons short, but I found out that, unlike Americans, Europeans don't expect or want a twenty-minute sermon. Especially in Russia, they come to listen for at least an hour and a half, and they don't want to leave feeling cheated. That's easy using an interpreter because it doubles the time. In Estonia, where half the people are Russian, the other half Estonian, preachers use two interpreters. First, the Russian interprets, then the Estonian interprets. But the message translates the same around the world.

I soon found that our move to Texas was very timely: Texas had 77,000 inmates, which by the end of the next year would top 140,000. With a backlog of 35,000 in the

What was your name in the club?

county jails, they had issued a "Macedonian Call": "Come over and help us."

Unknown to us, the Chairman of Texas Department of Criminal Justice Carroll Vance had said at a meeting of the wardens, "My goal is to see men saved in these prisons. I want you to go open the doors for the churches to come in and minister."

When we heard that, we were stunned that our move was so tremendously timely. The Chief Chaplain of the State, Jerry Groom, is a dear friend, so right away we found wide-open opportunities to minister in the state. As a result, we became more focused by discovering what questions the prisons were asking.

In Texas they were saying, "We want mentors, we want family ministry, drug and alcohol ministry, and literacy ministry." And, of course, we began developing programs right away.

Later in 1992, Pastor Charles Burton (VP of WVIW) and his wife Sharon accepted a special invitation from Frank Costantino, which resulted the next year in Charles' resigning from his church, and their moving to Estonia. Together, while they oversee the work at the prison hospital, they are also establishing Overcomers Groups in churches and prisons all over Estonia, and sponsoring a chaplaincy school.

Also in 1993, Gary and Charlotte Cook, traveling evangelists representing AVIW, heard from God that they were called to Belarus. When they discussed it with me, I said, "Go for it!"

They moved to Minsk, established a church, and almost immediately launched a weekly evangelistic program on TV. Right away, through a COPE Joint Venture with the Belarusan government, the Orthodox church of Belarus, and a church-planting ministry out of Amarillo, Texas, their original church in Minsk was able to

Delivered

pioneer three others. Also working a Joint Venture with WVIW, they opened a chaplaincy school on April 14, 1994, with twenty-five students being trained as chaplains for the nation. WVIW has also assumed responsibility for supporting one of those chapels, plus a year's salary for a Bible-school student when he becomes chaplain of an institution.

COPE members have also become active in Latvia, Hungary and Poland, where the Overcomers Program is well received and making a difference. The prison problem is not unique to America, even though the USA has recently passed South Africa as the number one country, incarcerating more people per 100,000 than any other nation in the world. But we find that prison culture everywhere is the same.

At home, our WVIW volunteer Bonny Scott coordinates our 500 volunteers in Texas, about the same number in Georgia, and again about the same number in all the other states in America, plus approximately 200 in Jamaica, including some who never go to prisons. She matches them up with what they want to do: teach, sing, stuff envelopes, write letters, etc. For banquets, for instance, she assigns little, easy jobs to about thirty volunteers, and that way the big jobs get done. Bonny Scott reports to my secretary, Mary Simmons.

Mary, who got involved with the ministry as a volunteer, assures me that God sent her my way because I needed her help in the office. She was right. Each morning, I tell her what needs to be done. Skilled at making decisions and delegating and creating jobs to make things happen, Mary brings it all together.

Early one morning in 1994, the phone rang, and I answered, "Worldwide Voice in the Wilderness."

"Is that Johnny Moffitt?"

"This is Johnny."

What was your name in the club?

"Did you once ride with the Bandidos?"
"Yeah! Who is this?"
"What year did you leave the club?"
"Sixty-nine."
"What was your name in the club?"
"Whale."
"Whale!? You're kidding! Do you know who this is?"
"No, who?"
"Tank!"
"You're kidding!"
"I ain't kidding! I left the club a few years ago, been driving a truck, now I'm here in Dallas. I started reading my Bible back in '86 in South Carolina. I'm a Christian now, man, and I wanta come by and see you!"
"Come on!"

Shortly afterwards, I opened the door to his knock. The guy on the other side filled the entire doorway. No doubt about it, it was Tank, now using his real name John.

"How do you like driving a truck?" I asked him.
"Not much. It's a job."
"Man, you don't need to be driving a truck. We can use you right here!"
"You're kidding!"
"I ain't kidding!"

As a result of that conversation, the Bandidos' former "demolition expert," now a new and gentle creature in Christ, ministers effectively in the prisons as one of our most popular guys representing WVIW, working with me side-by-side. He also often shows up at the office to do whatever Mary needs to have done. Only God could have arranged that.

My next vision is for Cuba. The first time I ever used an interpreter was in the Atlanta prison talking to the Cubans while being interpreted into Spanish.

I've been praying hard for Cuba, been collecting re-

Delivered

sources, and I always come back to the same criterion: I must have free access to a government official.

I recently got a letter of invitation from the Attorney General of Cuba, so we're now getting ready to hook up the phone calls. You can't call Cuba from the States because of our trade embargo, but I can hook up through Canada with a conference call.

We'll work out the dates, and then we're on our way to visit the prisons in Cuba—John and Johnny, a.k.a. Tank and Whale.

Hopefully, Jamaica will assume the business end of that venture...

By 1994, COPE claimed about 500 members strong worldwide, each ministry with its own circle of influence and relationships, extending into other countries on different continents, contacts ready-made for Joint Ventures with ministries yearning for something spiritual to happen while desperately needing the boost COPE can give to help set it off.

I expected international ministry to be different from what we were already doing, but basically it's the same. Prisoners are prisoners, the same in whatever society they are, and it's the same Good News of the Gospel of Jesus Christ that changes them.

CHAPTER TWENTY-FIVE

"What's the bottom line?"

[In Capernaum Jesus] was in the house. And ... many were gathered together, insomuch that there was no room to receive them ... and he preached the word unto them. And they came unto him bringing one sick of the palsy, which was borne of four. And when they could not come nigh unto him for the press, they uncovered the roof where he was: and when they had broken it up, they let down the bed wherein the sick of the palsy lay. When Jesus saw their faith, he said unto the sick of the palsy, Son, thy sins be forgiven thee. But there were certain of the scribes sitting there, and reasoning in their hearts, Why doth this man thus speak blasphemies? who can forgive sins but God only? And immediately when Jesus perceived in his spirit ... he said unto them, Why reason ye these things in your hearts? Whether is it easier to say ... Thy sins be forgiven thee; or to say, Arise, and take up thy bed, and walk? But that ye may know that the Son of man hath power to forgive sins, (he saith to the sick of the palsy,) I say unto thee, Arise, and take up thy bed, and go thy way into thine house. And immediately he arose, took up the bed, and went forth before them all; insomuch that they were all amazed, and glorified God, saying, We never saw it on this fashion.   Mark 2:1-12

In this Scripture passage Jesus goes to a home in Capernaum to rest. As usual, when everybody hears

Delivered

about it, they all pack in around Him, eight or ten deep, so nobody else can get in. When Jesus sees all the people, He begins to preach to them. But there's a man on a stretcher—paralyzed, as some translations say—and four of his friends take him to Jesus. When they can't even get on the porch, let alone inside, they rig some kind of block and tackle, hoist the guy up onto the roof, then get themselves up there someway. They chop hunks out of the roof, then lower the guy down through the big hole they made. That's the situation.

The first thing we see here is that the need is great. The guy on the stretcher is really sick. He can't heal himself, can't even walk. He really does need healing.

The need:

In our world too, the need for all kinds of healing is tremendous, especially in the prisons. Huge mission fields in this country are right at our doors.

Right now there are over 1,000,000 men, women and children locked up in American jails and prisons. In the United States one of every four black males between the ages of 18 and 25 is either in prison, on probation, or on parole. At any given time, you can call the jails across this country, and find that there are 500,000 men, women and children behind bars in our jails. That is my "man on the stretcher." They need to hear about Jesus.

The only way to change a man is to change his heart, and the only one who can do that is Jesus. That is the great need.

Real obstacles:

The second thing we see here is that the obstacles are real. Those were real people the four friends could not burrow through. That was a real roof they had to

What's the bottom line?

tear up. And they couldn't settle for a little hole, and let the guy on the stretcher down head or feet first. He'd slide right off the thing.

As Christians, sometimes we take somebody to Jesus, and drop him on his head right in front of Him—drop him and run. But those guys on the roof had to tear open a great, big hole.

In prison ministry the obstacles are real and many. But God says in His Word that we can "run through a troop and leap over a wall" (Psalm 18:29). We can overcome the obstacles, and one of the greatest is "security." We have to have it. Those concrete walls are real; those chain-link fences are real; that barbed wire is real; that guard with the gun and the stick on the side of his leg is real.

Prisoners don't just trot down the road to a Friday night worship service, and by and large you can't go there just any time to chat with them, either. But somebody can go in your place (Romans 10:14,15).

How does God break down the obstacles of security in the prison? By submission. Romans chapter 13 still says for us to be subject to the higher powers, not only to Christian higher powers. When we train prison ministers, we tell them over and over, "If the guard tells you to be out of there by 9 o'clock, do not come out of there at 9:10. Be out of there by 9 o'clock." The reason is that we want to be back in there the next week. God doesn't need for us to break their rules and stay later than the allotted time. He is big enough to continue to minister to that prisoner back in his cell after we are gone.

Lack of cooperation:

Another major obstacle is the uncooperative chaplain. In prisons across America not all chaplains are Christians.

Delivered

I said to one chaplain, "Brother, I want to be of assistance to your ministry. What can I do to help you? Bring materials? Supply you with a Bible teacher, or someone to come out here once a week to counsel or to share with the inmates? Send somebody out here to help with filing?"

He said, "I don't want anything religious in this prison." He was the chaplain, and he was an obstacle.

I received a letter addressed "To all Religious Volunteers." It said, "Inmates who have not professed a belief in the religion of the volunteer prior to their incarceration may voluntarily attend religious services, but the volunteer shall not initiate or attempt to convert such inmate to his beliefs."

That sounds like I'm allowed to preach, but not to preach. The great thing about that is that I don't preach religion. I don't convert anybody. All I do is teach what the Word of God says: that God forgives sins, and that Jesus loves these guys, as sorry as they are. That's freedom. I just teach and preach Jesus Christ: "Jesus loves you, He cares about you, and He's concerned about you. He knows what you have done, and He wants to forgive you, and love you." And through the power of the Holy Spirit, they just get saved all on their own.

The warden says, "That's fine, as long as you're not converting anybody."

False doctrines:

Another obstacle to the ministry is the cults. In our country we have freedom of religion: that means no matter what weirdo thing anybody wants to practice in prison, the inmate has the right to have his minister come and minister to him. That includes Islam, satanism, all the cults. But God is more powerful than all the cults

What's the bottom line?

together. "Greater is He that is within [me], than he that is in the world" (1 John 4:4).

On a Thursday night, Duane and I were ministering in a prison where there was a satanist church, but also a very strong, charismatic body of Christians. The chaplain came to me and said, "Johnny, there's a man in my office I want you to pray with."

We went into the office, and met the man who was a member of the satanist church, unable to sleep for three nights. All he thought about was how to kill himself. He just wanted to be free.

After we talked to him for about an hour, I said, "Brother, are you ready to let us pray for you?"

He said, "Yes, I am."

Duane bowed his head.

I said, "Brother, I want you to say this after me: 'In the name of Jesus . . .'"

When I said that, he jumped up and caught me with a right cross, and caught Duane with a left hook. Duane bounced off the bookshelf, and I rolled all the way over the chaplain's desk.

Now, this fellow weighed only about 130 pounds, and I'm full grown, but I rolled over that desk and hit the floor. But I got up and came back around. We began to minister deliverance to that man, and he got free and saved and baptized with the Holy Spirit. He became a leader in that Christian church in the prison, and is now a free man serving God on the outside. Jesus is powerful, powerful.

When Duane and I were driving back home that night, I said, "Duane, did you learn anything tonight?"

He said, "Yes, Johnny, I did. I learned that you do not close your eyes when you are praying for deliverance."

Delivered

Financing:

Another major obstacle we face is financing. Don't let anybody kid you that your tax dollars go to the prison chaplain's budget. No way! In most places the chaplain's budget is zero. With no budget, when a prison chaplain in Georgia needs a Bible for a prisoner, he has to call on another prison ministry—collect, because he is not allowed to make long-distance calls. In 1983, one chaplain submitted a request for $300 for a portable electric typewriter. He was turned down, and told not to ask again until 1984.

Praise God for Chaplain Ray, International Prison Ministries/Dallas, and the literature he sends out.

Praise God for Frank Costantino, Christian Prison Ministry/Orlando, and the video machines and tapes he places in the prisons to spread the gospel.

Culture shock:

Another major obstacle is culture shock. The guys we come to minister to come from a world different from ours. Many of them do not wash too often. They are just learning some other things they had never been taught. They talk a different language. Let me illustrate how different.

In 1979, one of Chuck Colson's Prison Fellowship groups went into a prison in North Carolina for a week-long seminar. On the last day the kingpin got saved. Then some of the other inmates, who had been watching him all week, went forward, too. If he could get saved, so could they. Now they had a church. The warden asked a lady named Jimi, who had already been working with the group, if she would come down each week and teach these men.

She said, "You bet!"

What's the bottom line?

The warden warned her that some of the guys coming out to the meetings might not be all that serious about the Lord, and that, in fact, one of them was a sex pervert. She was to keep her eyes open, and report to him if any of the prisoners made any move that he shouldn't make. So she started coming every week, sometimes bringing other Christians from town with her, and they would sing choruses and hymns, and worship the Lord, and study the Bible.

After about six weeks, the pervert made his move. But instead of telling the guard or the warden, Jimi told one of the "elders" of the inmate church. The elder in turn told the now-converted kingpin, who had taken over leadership of the inmate church, that he had a little matter of church discipline to take care of: One of the members of his congregation was not living quite holy. So, after the worship service, the leader called a meeting in the laundry room. After he told the other guys what had happened, they took a vote and it was unanimous—they would kill the guy.

That inmate church had a system that is almost scriptural: in Matthew 18, you give your erring brother three shots at it, right? Well, in prison, first they slap the guy's hand; then they work him over; then they kill him. This guy had his hand slapped a few times, been whipped a few times, so he was already living on grace. When he made his approach to Jimi, that was it.

After the decision was made, the leader decided that he had better notify the "apostle" of this work, so he wrote Chuck Colson a letter. Chuck dropped the letter and called the warden. When Jimi came the next week to teach, the guy had already been transferred to another camp.

Frank Costantino tells the classic culture-shock story of prison ministry, about the eager volunteer who had

Delivered

been ministering in a prison for about a year, and finally got his first convert. He ran and told his pastor, who said he would like to meet the guy. The following week the two of them were in the prison together when the new convert came up to them puffing on a cigarette. He blew smoke in their faces, and said, "Hello, there, preacher."

On the way home the preacher said to the volunteer, "I don't mean to be telling you how to run your ministry, but you need to teach that guy to quit smoking those cigarettes."

The young volunteer was quiet for about half a block, then said, "But first I've got to teach him to stop killing people."

First things first.

Prejudice:

One final obstacle to our ministry is racial prejudice. In Georgia about 65% of the prison population is black. If you are white and have the least tinge of prejudice, you cannot minister in that atmosphere. We know that "racial superiority" is a myth. If you have any trouble with that, read the first chapter of Ruth, Exodus 12:49, and Acts 13 (about a black apostle). Environment has a lot more to do with how a man acts than does his heredity.

In 1972, *"Time Magazine"* conducted what I consider to be one of the most significant surveys ever in the area of heredity vs. environment. They enlarged two photographs, one of a distinguished-looking man in a business suit, and the other of a hippie. Then they took them out to the streets to poll the people: "Which one of these two men would you consider the most trustworthy?"

Hands down, the man in the business suit won.

Six months later, they took the same two photographs into the same streets, and repeated the poll. This time the hippie won.

What's the bottom line?

What made the whole country change its mind in six months?

Watergate!

A man is not a criminal because he is black. A man is not a criminal because he is brown. A man is not a criminal because he is white. A man is a criminal because he robbed a filling-station. Somewhere along the line he said yes when he should have said no. We need to forget heredity, color and race, and just minister to the people.

Vocal critics:

My third point is this: Not only is the need great, not only are the obstacles real, but the critics are very vocal. Prison ministry is not the most popular ministry in the world. People are not standing in line to give their money to prison ministry.

Recently, I was giving my testimony to a group of citizens, when a man stood up and said, "Prisoners are getting exactly what they deserve." Then he turned around and walked out the door.

Remember what the Pharisees said, when Jesus told the man his sins were forgiven? They said, "Who does this guy think he is?"

Critics are also always worried about the cost. Can't you hear those Pharisees in Capernaum saying, "Who is going to pay for that roof?"

Why prison ministry?

Let me give you something very simple and very factual. Four out of five crimes are committed by ex-convicts. What does that mean to prison ministry? That means that if we reach twenty-five men this year—only twenty-five—then twenty crimes will not be committed. That means that twenty people will not go back to prison

Delivered

at a cost of over $15,000 per year for each one. That is a savings of over $300,000 a year from now on.

It costs the government between $35,000 and $75,000 per bed to build a new prison, and we need thousands of new beds to meet the present demand. But I am here today to submit to you that we don't need more prisons. What we need are changed lives. We need to reach these men with the power of the gospel of Jesus Christ. Then maybe we can begin to use the monstrosities they call prisons for old folks' homes, and children's homes, and things that are productive.

Four things never satisfied:

God has given me the or   ach every prison in the United States *effectively* with the full gospel message of Jesus Christ. How long am I going to preach this message? Proverbs chapter 30 says that there are four things that are never satisfied: the grave, the barren womb, the land without water, and the fire. So, I am going to quit preaching this when men quit dying, when women quit giving birth, when the desert stops sucking up water, and when the fire quits burning in my soul. And that will not happen until I have reached every prison in the United States of America and in as many countries as the Lord opens doors, *effectively*, with the gospel of Jesus Christ.

The needs are great.

The obstacles are great.

The critics are very vocal.

But note the bottom line in the above Scripture passage: The guy gets healed.